Joe Stahlkuppe

Great Danes

Everything about Purchase, Care, Nutrition,
Breeding, Behavior, and Training
with 46 color photos

Drawings by Michele Earle-Bridges
Consulting Editor: Matthew M. Vriends, Ph.D.

BARRON'S

Contents

Preface

The Great Dane has been partially misnamed, since the breed isn't Danish at all, but the "great" part is certainly right on target. Great Dane enthusiasts know all the perils of owning a pony-sized dog and still they persevere. While all breeds have strong adherents and supporters, no breed can boast more solid backers than the Great Dane. It is my unabashed belief that the Great Dane has some of the finest or "greatest" people in all of the purebred dog hobby. My only question is: did the great people gravitate to the great dogs, or did the dogs become great because of the people involved?

I owe much to my wife and partner Cathie for her encouragement and assistance. I also owe my son Shawn and his wife Lisa for their help during this project. Many thanks go to Fred R. Jackson, Willard Stringer, and Frank Stahlkuppe for their years of support and friendship.

Old friends to be mentioned are Malcolm B. Street, Jr., Larry Smith, Edward M. George, William "Buddy" McLeroy, Bert Alexander, Jr., and Ken Jones. In a book about Great Danes, great friends are totally appropriate. I would also like to share the memory of Polly Alexander, Vicki Alexander, Don Wilkinson, and Joe Hulon. There have been a large number of Great Dane fans who have contributed to this small book about a giant dog: some of them are Cathie Abbott, Ginger Jones, Cynthia Bonnett, Jeanette and Lori Pickett, Bob and Kay Thompson, Dr. Gary Jones, Conni Borwick, and Valerie Clows, all of whom share the view that "Danes Are Great!"

Joe Stahlkuppe

Great Danes: An Introduction

The Size Factor

This book has a recurring theme—"Giant dogs bring giant responsibilities!" It is crucial that any Dane owner or prospective Dane owner understand this. Although ownership of a Great Dane can be immensely pleasurable, ownership of a dog of a giant breed requires extra thought, planning, and care. The normal situations and circumstances confronting every dog owner are magnified when the dog stands a yard (1 m) high at the shoulder and weighs as much as or more than the owner.

Almost every aspect of Great Dane ownership is affected by the size factor. Forgetting this factor in even one instance can have unpleasant or even

Adult Great Danes possess both power and elegance in large portions.

disastrous consequences. For example, an experienced dog breeder who lived in the southern United States and kept a number of beagles for hunting, purchased a harlequin Great Dane puppy as a pet. The young Dane was developing into an excellent companion dog and she was much loved by the entire household. The rapidly growing dog was allowed access to both the house and a large fenced backyard. On short, overnight family trips, the young Dane was put in a large, fenced kennel area where several beagles also lived. A large, multi-dog dog house was available for all the dogs if the weather was chilly or rainy. Having grown up with the beagles, the Dane pup would simply follow the other dogs inside the large dog house. The body heat of several dogs and beds of clean straw made for a comfortable abode.

Because this kenneling arrangement had always worked well, the family went away for an overnight trip, secure in the assumption that upon their return all the animals would be in their usual good shape. A sudden storm front, rare in that part of the country, plunged temperatures below 0° Fahrenheit (−17°C) for about 12 hours. The family returned home to find the beagles in excellent condition and the young Dane frozen to death. She had grown so rapidly that she could no longer fit through the dog house door, and her short-haired coat could not protect her from

The time to teach puppies the right things is before they stand a yard high at the shoulder and weigh over 100 pounds.

the cold. Giant dogs bring giant responsibilities.

Meet the Great Dane

It may seem unnecessary to introduce readers to what is one of the most recognizable dog breeds in the world, but the Great Dane many people think they know may not be the real Great Dane at all! Dane breeders and owners point out that their calf-size pets attract a lot of attention when out in public—on walks, at shows, and so forth. People who wouldn't think of commenting on a Doberman or a German shepherd often approach Dane owners with questions about the dog, its size, how much it eats, and so on. The Great Dane is an attention-getter.

Sensitivity: What many casual observers do not know is that the huge, perhaps even awe-inspiring dog has a host of other attributes that make it a unique pet. For example, under the big, tough exterior, Great Danes are often quite sensitive. Some owners report that an unintentionally loud reprimand can cause a Dane to go to a safe area in the home and withdraw for lengthy periods of time.

An amusing story that points out both the size factor and the sensitivity of some Danes concerns a large, brindle male and a small toddler. The big dog had been with the family for several years before the child was born. After coming to learn about the new little girl, the Dane became devoted to the child. The little girl learned to stand by pulling herself up and holding onto the dog. Soon, she was taking unsteady steps using the Dane as a moving support, a role the big guy seemed to relish.

Danes often lean against their humans, and the dog did this with the wobbly little girl, causing her to fall down. One day the child, who was also learning to talk at about the same time, took a tumble because of the dog. Pulling herself up by grabbing the Dane firmly on both sides of his large muzzle, the child looked the dog straight in the eye and proceeded in unintelligible baby jabber to berate the careless canine. When she had had her say, she went on to some other activity. Later, the child's parents found the deeply chastened Dane in his crate looking very sad indeed. It was hours before the dog would come near the child, who had already forgotten the incident.

Malleability: Another Dane trait that may not be widely known is their high degree of malleability. Long-time fans of the breed assert that Great Danes can become spoiled, aggressive, or even too passive if their humans allow them to become so. Great Danes have done well in obedience trials, the show ring, and schutzhund work, and as pets. The key to successful Dane development seems clearly to be the dog's owners. A cruel owner who habitually mistreats a Dane could get a dangerous dog for his or her efforts. A lazy owner who will not take control and help a Great Dane become a good pet may get a stubborn dog that tries to dominate its humans. An owner who obtains a good-quality Great Dane from a reputable source, plans and prepares for the dog, then cares for and trains the Dane can reasonably expect to get a super-sized pet that will be the equal of any other dog of any other breed as an individual or family companion.

Physical Appearance

Perhaps because of its distinctive appearance, the Great Dane has often been featured in books, on television, in the movies, and even in the comics section of newspapers. Companies have cashed in on the instant-recognition value of the dog's image and name. As a result, some

Four of the five currently accepted colors of Great Dane: blue, harlequin, fawn, and brindle. Each of these colors, and also the black Dane, has its own fans, who believe that their favorite color is the most beautiful.

uninformed people have developed mental pictures of the Dane as either a huge, dangerous creature to be feared and avoided or a buffoonish, clownlike caricature of a dog. Neither perception is accurate. A mistreated Great Dane chained to the bumper of a wrecked car in a junkyard could indeed be unhappy and overly aggressive. A Dane puppy can be a humorous image of overstated feet, legs, and ears. But a Great Dane given great care, great training, and great affection will usually become a great pet!

With its combination of elegance and power, the Great Dane is almost a contradiction in terms. It is muscular without the heavy bulkiness of the mastiff, Saint Bernard, or Newfoundland, yet with more substance to go with its height than the Irish wolfhound. The Dane's regal bearing often has been portrayed in sculpture and paintings.

As one American Kennel Club judge stated, "Even a relatively poor-quality Dane by show standards can still be quite an impressive animal." Many written descriptions of the Great Dane included in the kennel club standards of various nations call the breed the "Apollo of the dog world." Moreover, the Great Dane's powerful, elegant frame can be found in any one of several colors, each with a group of fans proclaiming it the most attractive.

Coat Colors

In the United States, Great Danes currently have five accepted colors in their standard, the "breed blueprint" drawn up by experts and serving as the basis for the placing of awards in American Kennel Club sanctioned dog shows. The acceptable show colors are:

Fawn: This is the popular light tan to reddish tan that is often seen in Great Danes.

Harlequin (standing) matings will sometimes produce colors not accepted by the AKC. Among these are the "Boston" or mantled Dane and the merle Dane. While dogs of these off-colors may be excellent pets, they are not to be considered especially rare. Merles are usually spayed or neutered.

Owning a Great Dane means not just owning a big dog, but owning a GIANT dog.

The merle Dane, while attractive, should be considered a non-breedable pet only.

Brindle: Brindle is essentially a fawn coat with irregular black stripes over the fawn background.

Black: The black Dane is at its best when the black is deep and solid in color, free of white and without a reddish or yellowish cast.

Blue: A blue Dane has a gun-metal-colored coat without other colors or white to affect the total impression of a large deep-smoke-colored dog.

Harlequin: Acknowledged as perhaps the most difficult color to breed correctly in all of dogdom and unique to Great Danes, a harlequin is a white dog with irregular small patching of black in a symmetrical pattern all over its body. The harlequin color differs from the Dalmatian pattern in that the Great Dane pattern is marked with jagged, irregular patches of differing sizes. The Dalmatian, which was once incorrectly classified as a small version of the harlequin Great Dane, has regular roundish spots of nearly the same uniform size.

In addition to the five accepted colors, the Great Dane can appear in some other colors in pet quality only.

"Boston": This pattern got its name from a resemblance to the black and white collar, front, and feet of the Boston terrier. Most often Bostons are a by-product of harlequin breedings. Bostons can be quite attractive and are accepted as show colors in Canada and Europe. It is possible that the Great Dane Club of America will soon officially accept this color, possibly to be called "mantled." Good Bostons are sometimes used in harlequin breeding.

Merle: Like the "Boston," the merle can result from attempts to breed harlequins. The merle is usually a bluish-gray base color with irregular black markings sprinkled on the coat. The merle should never be used in breeding. (Some Dane breeders routinely destroy all merle puppies as they are born; others offer them for sale as pets only.)

Other nonaccepted colors:
Sometimes Danes, especially those indiscriminately mated among the color varieties, produce solid white dogs, white dogs with irregular patches of fawn, blue, or brindle, and even "Boston" or mantled-pattern dogs in blue or brindle or fawn. Dogs of these colors are usually eliminated as newborns. Occasionally, some are passed as pets.

Summary: Only the five standard colors—fawn, brindle, black, blue, and harlequin—are accepted by the American Kennel Club. While the "Boston" may have breeding value in the hands of a harlequin expert, the merle and other "off-colors" are not rare nor are they valuable except as pets. Breeders who do not humanely destroy such pups sell them at reduced prices to people who will spay or neuter these unacceptably colored dogs.

History of the Great Dane

We do not know precisely when the breed originated. We do know that dogs resembling Danes have been in the company of humans for hundreds of years. Although some British breed authorities disagree, the Great Dane appears to be largely a German creation, one in which Germany takes considerable pride. It is also true that a dog very similar to the Great Dane was evolving in England and that modern Danes probably owe some debt to these early British dogs in addition to the German contributions to the breed.

The ancestors of the Great Dane were most likely of hunting stock. Since the Dane is a taller, slimmer counterpart to the English mastiff, it is probable that some mastiff genetic material found its way into the breed. The Dane was for a time called the "German mastiff," a name that was only partially accurate and that failed to catch on.

Not yet an AKC-recognized color, "Boston" or "mantled" Danes can still be beautiful and make excellent pets.

There are several attractive colors in Great Danes. Shown here are a harlequin, a Boston, and a brindle.

English sources believe that the Dane is a British product that the Germans improved and developed to a high level. These sources hypothesize that the Dane arose as a cross between the large, heavy mastiff and the speedy, trimmer greyhound. The Germans also had a pre-Dane mastiff-type dog of their own, the "bullenbeisser." This large, rough ancestor of both the German Dane and the boxer was somewhat lighter than its English cousin. It is thought that the "bullenbeisser" and the English mastiff were used in similar crosses with swifter, lighter dogs, like the greyhound or deerhound, that gave greater speed to the resulting offspring.

Still other references make a case for the Great Dane as being descended, at least in part, from the ancient Irish wolfhound crossed with the mastiff. The modern Irish wolfhound comes the closest of any breed in resembling the modern Great Dane. It is interesting that when the Irish breed was near extinction around the turn of the century, the Great Dane was used to add new genetic material to the few wolfhound lines still in existence.

That the Germans first recognized the value of a dog like the Great Dane and seized the opportunity to make the assorted dogs of this type into a breed is undeniably true. The Great Dane of today owes much to the Germans who created the first standard for the breed, then followed it strictly.

Great Danes, in whatever country, were originally hunting dogs, used especially on the fearsome, dangerous European wild boars. These boars, which had little resemblance to barnyard porkers, were a tough and potentially deadly prey requiring a dog of courage, speed, and exceptional power. The early Danes fit this model and succeeded admirably at the task.

The large boarhound made the transition from purely sporting dog to protective guard dog. This change, which took place quite gradually, required attributes other than the ability to hunt boars. Protection dogs need to be more people-oriented, of less violent temperament, amenable to tasks other than the chase, and equipped with the capacity to live in reasonably close proximity to people.

Almost from its beginning as a recognized breed, the Great Dane, or "Deutsch Dogge," was embraced by the dog breeders and citizens of Germany. Many well-known Germans have owned Great Danes. Notably, Otto von Bismarck loved Great Danes and did much to further the breed. The fabled German aviator Manfred von Richthofen, the "Red Baron" of World War I, owned a Great Dane named Max. He would often put the big dog in the second seat of his plane and take the Dane up into the world of early manned flight.

Germans continue to place stringent requirements on the breeding, care, and training of the "Deutsche Dogge." By setting tough rules and adhering to them, breeders have ensured that the Dane would be not only a large, elegant dog, but also a powerful and useful one.

What's in a Name?

Over the centuries the breed we now call the Great Dane has had perhaps dozens of names, some more appropriate and accurate than others. Originally thought of as and called a boarhound, the big German dog was also called an "Ulmer" hound or dog. As mentioned, the name German mastiff was used for a time. "Tiger" dog, perhaps referring to the striping of the brindle or even the patching of the harlequin, was a name at one time attached to the breed.

One fact is clear: The Great Dane is in no way Danish! For some reason now lost in the past, the French naturalist Buffon referred to this breed as the "Grande Danois" or "big Dane" and this name, although still not used in Europe, was adopted by the English-speaking world.

Popularity for the Great Dane has not come without a price. For some people a type of "bigger is better" attitude has caused the Dane to be the dog of choice, without much forethought. The idea of owning the biggest dog in the neighborhood seems to captivate some people. The fact that having the biggest dog will bring additional costs, responsibilities, and possibly additional problems is not always considered.

As puppies, Great Danes have much the same appeal as puppies of many other breeds. A young Dane brought into an unprepared home may do very well for the first weeks or months. Even during this period, however, a fast-growing Dane puppy needs more attention to its nutritional needs than dogs of some smaller breeds. A young Great Dane can weigh more than most children. When such a puppy jumps up on a child, the child is probably going to fall down. When such a puppy's whiplike tail is happily wagging, items on coffee tables are going to be swept right off. When such a puppy runs, in the usually clumsy fashion of most puppies, things in its path have a way of being bowled over.

It is sad that some families decide the biggest dog in the neighborhood is too much dog for them while the young Dane is still a puppy. Sometimes people who have bought a Great Dane puppy as an impressive status-symbol-in-the-making relegate the dog to the backyard, to a small kennel area, to a friend who lives in the country, or even to the city pound. Although the Great Dane puppy has done only what it should be expected to do as a Great Dane puppy, the sensitive young dog can be cast aside by owners who were more interested in impressing the neighbors than in adding a living, breathing pet to the family. As one veteran Dane breeder stated, "If all these people want is something large and impressive, let them get a statue of a dog instead of a dog itself." Giant dogs bring giant responsibilities.

American Kennel Club Standard

General appearance: In its regal appearance, the Great Dane combines dignity, strength, and elegance with great size and a powerful, well-formed, smoothly muscled body. It is one of the giant working breeds, but is unique in that its general conformation must be so well balanced that it never appears clumsy, and shall move with a long reach and powerful drive. It is always a unit—the Apollo of dogs. A Great Dane must be spirited, courageous, never timid; always friendly and dependable. This physical and mental combination is the characteristic that gives the Great Dane the majesty possessed by no other breed. It is particularly true of this breed that there is an impression of great masculinity in dogs, as compared to an impression of femininity in bitches. Lack of true Dane breed type, as defined in this standard, is a serious fault.

Size, proportion, substance: The male should appear more massive throughout than the bitch, with larger frame and heavier bone. In the ratio between length and height, the Great Dane should be square. In bitches, a somewhat longer body is permissible, providing she is well proportioned to her height. Coarseness or lack of substance are equally undesirable. The male shall not be less than 30 inches (76 cm) or more, but it is preferable that he be 32 inches (82 cm) or more, providing he is well proportioned to his height. The female

The fawn Great Dane is a favorite with many fans of the breed.

shall not be less than 28 inches (71 cm) at the shoulders, but it is preferable that she be 30 inches (76 cm) or more, providing she is well propor-

This head study of a Great Dane shows an almost regal bearing. Notice the ears are cropped.

tioned to her height. Danes under minimum height must be disqualified.

Head: The head shall be rectangular, long, distinguished, expressive, finely chiseled, especially below the eyes. Seen from the side, the Dane's forehead must be sharply set off from the bridge of the nose (a strongly pronounced stop). The plane of the skull and the plane of the muzzle must be straight and parallel to one another. The skull plane under and to the inner point of the eyes must slope without any bony protuberance in a smooth line to a full square jaw with a deep muzzle (fluttering lips are undesirable). The masculinity of the male is very pronounced in the structural appearance of the head. The bitch's head is more delicately formed. Seen from the top, the skull should have parallel sides and the bridge of the nose should be as broad as possible. The cheek muscles should not be prominent. The length from the tip of the nose to the center of the stop should be equal to the length from the center of the stop to the rear

This powerful brindle clearly shows why the Great Dane has been called "the Apollo of the dog world."

of the slightly developed occiput. The head should be angular from all sides and should have flat planes with dimensions in proportion to the size of the Dane. Whiskers may be trimmed or left natural.

Eyes shall be medium-size, deep-set, and dark, with a lively, intelligent expression. The eyelids are almond-shaped and relatively tight, with well-developed brows. Haws and mongolian eyes are serious faults. In harlequins, the eyes should be dark; light-colored eyes, eyes of different colors, and walleyes are permitted but not desirable. Ears shall be high set, medium in size, and of moderate thickness, folded forward close to the cheek. The top line of the folded ear should be level with the skull. If cropped, the ear length is in proportion to the size of the head and the ears are carried uniformly erect. Nose shall be black, except in the blue Dane, where it is a dark blue-black. A black spotted nose is permitted on the harlequin; a pink-colored nose is not desirable. A split nose is a disqualifica-

tion. Teeth shall be strong, well-developed, clean, and with full dentition. The incisors of the lower jaw touch very lightly the bottoms of the inner surface of the upper incisors (scissor bites).

This Dane's ears are uncropped and yet the dog is still quite impressive.

An undershot jaw is a very serious fault. Overshot or wry bites are serious faults. Even bites, misaligned or crowded incisors are minor faults.

Neck, topline, body: The neck shall be firm, high set, well arched, long, and muscular. From the nape, it should gradually broaden and flow smoothly into the withers. The neck underline should be clean. Withers shall slope smoothly into a short level back with a broad loin. The chest shall be broad, deep, and well muscled. The forechest should be well developed without a pronounced sternum. The brisket extends to the elbow, with well-sprung ribs. The body underline should be tightly muscled with a well-defined tuck-up. The croup should be broad and very slightly sloping. The tail should be set high and smoothly into the croup, but not quite level with the back, a continuation of the spine. The tail should be broad at the base, tapering uniformly down to the hock joint. At rest, the tail should fall straight. When excited or running, it may curve slightly, but never above the level of the back. A ring or hooked tail is a serious fault. A docked tail is a disqualification.

Forequarters: The forequarters, viewed from the side, shall be strong and muscular. The shoulder blade must be strong and sloping, forming, as near as possible, a right angle in its articulation with the upper arm. A line from the upper tip of the shoulder to the back of the elbow joint should be perpendicular. The ligaments and muscles holding the shoulder blade to the rib cage must be well developed, firm, and securely attached to prevent loose shoulders. The shoulder blade and the upper arm should be the same length. The elbow should be one-half the distance from the withers to the ground. The strong pasterns should slope slightly. The feet should be round and compact with well-arched toes, neither toeing in, toeing out, nor rolling to the inside or outside. The nails should be short, strong, and as dark as possible, except that they may be lighter in harlequins. Dewclaws may or may not be removed.

Hindquarters: The hindquarters shall be strong, broad, muscular, and well angulated, with well let down hocks. Seen from the rear, the hock joints appear to be perfectly straight, turning neither toward the inside nor toward the outside. The rear feet should be round and compact, with well-arched toes, neither toeing in nor out. The nails should be short, strong, and as dark as possible, except they may be lighter in harlequins. Wolf claws are a serious fault.

Coat: The coat shall be short, thick, and clean with a smooth, glossy appearance.

Color, Markings, and Patterns

Brindle: The base color shall be yellow gold and always brindled with strong black cross stripes in a chevron pattern. A black mask is preferred. Black should appear on the eye rims and eyebrows, and may appear on the ears and tail tip. The more intensive the base color and the more distinct and even the brindling, the more preferred will be the color. Too much or too little brindling are equally undesirable. White markings at the chest and toes, black-fronted, dirty-colored brindles are not desirable.

Fawn: The color shall be yellow gold with a black mask. Black should appear on the eye rims and eyebrows, and may appear on the ears and tail tip. The deep yellow gold must always be given the preference. White markings at the chest and toes, black-fronted, dirty-colored fawns are not desirable.

Blue: The color shall be a pure steel blue. White markings at the chest and toes are not desirable.

Black: The color shall be a glossy black. White markings at the chest and toes are not desirable.

Harlequin: Base color shall be pure white with black torn patches irregularly and well distributed over the entire body; a pure white neck is preferred. The black patches should never be large enough to give the appearance of a blanket, nor so small as to give a stipple or dappled effect. Eligible, but less desirable, are a few small gray patches, or a white base with single black hairs showing through, which tend to give a salt-and-pepper or dirty effect.

Any variance in color or markings as described above shall be faulted to the extent of the deviation. Any Great Dane which does not fall within the above color classifications must be disqualified.

Gait: The gait denotes strength and power with long, easy strides resulting in no tossing, rolling, or bouncing of the topline or body. The backline shall appear level and parallel to the ground. The long reach should strike the ground below the nose while the head is carried forward. The powerful rear drive should be balanced to the reach. As speed increases, there is a natural tendency for the legs to converge toward the centerline of balance beneath the body. There should be no twisting in or out at the elbow or hock joints.

Temperament: The Great Dane must be spirited, courageous, always friendly and dependable, and never timid or aggressive.

* * *

The Great Ear Controversy

To crop or not to crop—that is the question for some Great Dane enthusiasts. The practice of trimming Great Danes' ears is called cropping, and strong voices argue for and against it.

Originally, when the Great Dane was the boarhound, its ears were cropped to protect them from the tusks of the large wild boars that were the hunting breed's principal prey. Later, as the boarhound became the Great Dane, the aristocratic look of the cropped ears was kept more as an attractive feature than as a hunting precaution. The original cropping for Danes was somewhat similar to that seen on American pit bull terriers and American Staffordshire terriers. Later, what became known as the "long crop" became fashionable, and it is this version that many Great Danes display today.

Anti-cropping sentiment arose in England when the Prince of Wales (later King Edward VII) came out strongly against cropped ears. The sovereign's will endured and Dane ear cropping ceased within the British Isles, much to the dismay of Dane breeders who thought the cropped ears added greatly to the look of their favorite breed.

Whether or not to crop a Dane's ears is its owner's decision. While cropped ears are not mandatory in the AKC standard, most experts believe uncropped dogs have more difficulty winning in the show ring.

Cropped ears, to be at their best, must be cropped and bandaged by a skilled veterinarian who knows how to do them.

Ear cropping is still the norm for Great Danes of show quality in the United States. While the AKC standard for the breed does not oppose the practice, Dane fanciers—both proponents and opponents of cropping—admit that an uncropped dog has a harder road in tough breed competition than its equal with cropped ears.

As of now, the decision rests in your hands. If you are going to have the cropping done, the best time for a healthy puppy to undergo the procedure is after seven weeks of age. Cropping should be done by a skilled veterinarian who is experienced specifically with Dane ear cropping and comfortable with the practice. If this description does not fit your veterinarian, perhaps your fellow Dane fanciers could recommend someone with the appropriate ability and background.

A poor cropping job can spoil a pup's chances as a show dog. After their ears are cropped, the puppies must be stoutly bandaged and kept from doing themselves harm by pawing at their still-tender ears. To crop or not to crop is your decision, but if you elect to have it done, by all means see that it is done correctly. Even with a skilled surgeon, cropped ears may not always stand completely erect because of the structure of the ears on a particular Dane puppy, poor bandaging, or other factors that can affect the appearance of the ears.

Elizabethan collars keep the pups' ears protected during the first days after cropping.

Understanding the Great Dane

When a dog is nearly a yard (1 m) high at the shoulder and would tower over all but the tallest humans when standing on its hind legs, its size can become the most significant factor for some people. It is certainly true that the Great Dane possesses impressive size, but it is not size alone that makes the Great Dane great. The regal bearing, expressive face, and dignity of the dog make it memorable along with its grand proportions.

To understand the Great Dane, one must understand the centuries of human contact that have gone into forming the breed. The Great Dane was once a hunting dog, faster than the mastiff and more powerful than the greyhound, but with aspects of both these ancient breeds. In the forerunners of the Dane, the boarhounds, temperament was often of secondary importance; the dogs were bred primarily for the savagery of the hunt.

When the big dogs began to attract attention as more than mere hunters and gain appeal as guards and companions, the aggressive nature of the boarhound had to be modified into a more placid, yet still watchful demeanor. As the early Great Dane breeders solidified the breed type, they persisted in trying to produce a big, alert dog that would be safe around people and other animals. A Great Dane with the overly aggressive nature of some terriers would have been a liability.

Taking the rough boarhound and transforming it into an elegant dog that would conform to palace or manor house was not the easiest of tasks. Even such noted Dane owners as Otto von Bismarck occasionally had dogs that needed close watching to keep them from being too protective. When the first dog shows began to take place, Great Danes were often so surly that the breed suffered from negative publicity. But through it all, the dedicated Dane breeders worked to produce a temperamentally sound breed. The modern Great Dane is the

Great Danes are more than just elegant giants. For the right owners, they make excellent family pets.

end result of long years of strict selective breeding. By carefully seeking a Great Dane from stock noted for good temperament and then following through with adequate training, today's potential Dane owner should find this giant better behaved than many other breeds.

The Nature of the Breed

Great Dane breeders often point out that the big dogs are generally quite sensitive. To non-Dane fanciers, the idea that a huge canine could get its feelings hurt by words alone seems humorous, if not unbelievable. That a dog weighing over 130 pounds (58.5 kg) could be more sensitive than some of the toy breeds weighing less than 5 pounds (2.25 kg) seems improbable, yet it is often the case.

Although this sensitivity definitely does exist, it would be an error to brand the breed as giant softies or pushovers. There are, as one well-known breeder stated, as many kinds of Great Danes as there are kinds of dogs. Occasionally a Dane has all the aggressive tendencies of breeds noted more for their guard and attack work. Some Danes are sedentary, with lives defined in terms of eating, sleeping, watching television, and the like. Some Danes show marked abilities not necessarily in keeping with their historical and genetic heritage. One big fawn male served as a very adequate retriever for his gamebird-hunting master. Still other Danes abhor the sound of gunfire. There are smart Great Danes and those not quite as smart. Some Great Danes do well in obedience trials. Others are better suited for other activities. One blue female was fond of accompanying her dairy farmer owner as he brought in the cows for milking. Like many collies and other farm shepherds before her, this Dane gradually became able to do the herding on her own.

Blue is another of the accepted Great Dane colors.

Some Great Danes have a fondness for "showbiz." Over the years, although no "Lassie," "Rin-Tin-Tin," or "Benji" has emerged, Great Danes have been featured in a number of films. One Disney film showed the dog's comedic flair when a Great Dane raised with a group of dachshunds came to believe that it was a dachshund too! Another Dane participated in annual Christmas parades in disguise, wearing a pair of reindeer antlers. The owner was convinced that the Dane found most of the parade boring, except when the dog's float passed the cheering crowds. Then the Dane became alert and seemed to enjoy the public adulation.

Never leave a Great Dane alone in a situation like this. Too many unexpected things can happen—all of them bad.

Illustrating the clown spirit hiding inside most Danes, this harlequin tries to bury her soccer ball.

A well-trained Great Dane from a good genetic background can be an excellent pet in a home where the humans are knowledgeable and well prepared. "Such a dog can become," as one longtime Dane breeder stated, "a family legend that you tell your grandchildren about." The same breeder also pointed out that a poorly bred, ill-trained Great Dane in the hands of an ignorant or neglectful owner can also be quite memorable— but for entirely different reasons!

Great Danes as Family Pets

A Great Dane can be an excellent addition to a family that wants a really big canine member and is willing to take responsibility for a bigger-than-big dog. For a single person with adequate time to give a Great Dane the care and training it will need, a Dane is also a good choice. But for a family or individual who wants a dog only as a fashion statement or living burglar alarm, a Great Dane is a horrible choice.

The Dane with the best chance to become a successful pet is the one with the most opportunity for close interaction with humans. Great Danes exiled to the kennel or the backyard for days or weeks on end become kennel and yard dogs whose personalities do not advance past a certain stage. They remain big dogs out back who eat, sleep, relieve themselves, bark, then start the cycle over again. To sentence any dog, especially a Great Dane, to such a life is a subtle but definite form of abuse.

Great Danes can become good family members, aware of their place in the family hierarchy and fitting into most of the family activities. While a large house with a large, fenced yard would be the best situation for any giant dog, Great Danes given adequate training and exercise can share urban settings with their owners. The degree to which a family is successful in owning a Great Dane is directly proportional to the level of commitment the family is willing to give.

Great Danes in Obedience Work

Great Danes are not seen in obedience trials as frequently as German shepherds, golden retrievers, and other breeds. A number of Danes, however, have done very well in their pursuit of obedience titles.

Obedience trials licensed by the AKC offer the following titles for the dogs and owners who are willing to put in the training time to learn an increasingly difficult group of tasks: Companion Dog (C.D.); Companion Dog Excellent (C.D.X.); and Utility Dog (U.D.). Obedience titles are placed after the dog's name, as in Baron von Bismarck of York, C.D. Guidelines explaining what is required and how to get involved in obedience trials are available from the AKC (see Useful Addresses and Literature, page 92).

While most dogs can be improved with appropriate training, training is essential for a dog the size of a Great Dane. In regular training, as in obedience work, the dog must be under the control of a human being and not the other way around. Obedience trial training and involvement for a Great Dane and its owner can be a very rewarding experience, but also a frustrating one. Not every dog is a good candidate for the discipline and hard work required to be successful in AKC licensed obedience trials. Every Great Dane should learn to obey basic commands (see Training Your Great Dane, page 48), even those that don't participate with their owners in obedience trials.

Great Danes as Show Dogs

A famous breeder and exhibitor of harlequin Great Danes once suggested, "Perhaps one reason that this breed does so well in the show ring may be that Great Danes are always on exhibition in one form or another."

The Great Dane has an appearance, a presence, and a demeanor that make it a natural for the show ring.

Danes do seem to attract a lot of attention, even when they are just out for a walk with their owners. Strangers who would not dream of going up to a beagle or poodle owner will not only stop, but also ask a lot of questions about a Great Dane. Even at dog shows where Great Danes are often seen, a really excellent specimen will attract the attention of viewers who would never classify themselves as Great Dane enthusiasts.

Unlike some of the other breeds in the AKC working dog group, the Great Dane really didn't begin to arouse interest until the advent of dog show. That Great Danes have done well in competition is evidenced by the number of champions the breed has produced and the number of top prizes Danes have won. The Great Dane and the show ring seem to have a definite affinity for one another.

Great Danes as Guard Dogs

The Great Dane is an impressive guard dog if it stands still and barks. It is probably this deterring factor that is the best aspect of the Great Dane as a guard dog breed. Certainly some do reasonably well in guard and attack dog training, but Danes don't seem to relish such work as thoroughly as Dobermans, Rottweilers, and some other breeds. That Danes are less often seen in the schutzhund competitions where trained dogs attack well-padded "enemies" is probably a relief to the people who wear the pads. Great Danes may not take to guard and attack work as readily as some other breeds, but when motivated to attack, a Great Dane is an awesome, damaging force.

The Great Dane will function best as a personal guard for you and your family if it is a genuine part of the family. A booming bark and the none-too-subtle sound of the heavy footfalls of a rapidly approaching huge dog are enough to frighten away all but the most determined (or the most stupid) of criminals.

Great Danes that have been rejected by their first owners sometimes end up as guard dogs in a store or a junkyard. These Danes were either poorly bred pets with uncertain temperaments or family dogs from neglectful families. For whatever reason, relegating Danes to such lives is a sad indictment of the breeders or families that let this happen.

If you want a live-in pet that will give its life to protect you, a Great Dane is a good choice. If you want an attack dog solely as a guard, do yourself and a Great Dane a favor—choose something else!

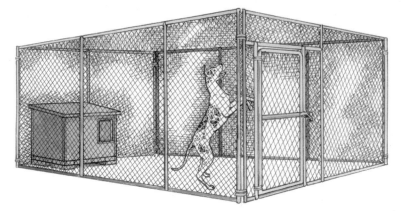

Living With a Great Dane

"Great" Means Bigger Than Big

An adult Great Dane is much larger than a German shepherd, a collie, or even a Rottweiler, all breeds appropriately thought of as "big" dogs. At maturity, most Great Danes will be easily able to put their chins on the average table. The length of the average Dane's body when full grown will exceed, when the tail is included, the height of most adult human males. Such a long body requires sufficient turning and maneuvering space in a home, in a kennel, a run, or a yard.

The weight of the average adult Great Dane equals that of most teenagers and many adult humans.

The harlequin Great Dane is predominantly white with irregular black patches over a large part of its body.

This weight is distributed over four legs, somewhat more delicate in structure than the two legs that would support a human being who weighed the same amount. A large Great Dane can occupy much more space on a couch (if it is allowed on a couch) than two average-size humans.

The Dane's tail is a mighty whip that in one swish can sweep a coffee table clean of china cups or bric-a-brac. It can knock a toddler down with the enthusiastic wagging such a child is likely to elicit from most friendly Great Danes. A Great Dane that jumps up on people (a very bad habit to allow any dog to learn) can topple large children and small adults. The toenails of an excitable Dane puppy can rake furrows across furniture or the human skin. Add to the physical aspects of Dane ownership the fact that these dogs are fond of leaning on people and things, whether or not the things or people are capable of supporting such demonstrative affection. Older people and children need to realize that Danes like to be physically next to the people they love; they have to brace themselves for the onslaught of an adoring dog. While Danes do not usually experience the excessive drooling of mastiffs, Saint Bernards, and other breeds, some Great Danes do drool enough to make their saliva a threat to furniture maintenance and sanitary conditions.

Although these physical traits would seem to make the Dane a purely out-

This older Dane shows great patience, but children should always be supervised around dogs, mostly for the dogs' sakes.

side pet, that should not be your conclusion. Great Danes certainly enjoy time outside every day for walks in a yard or a kennel run, but they adore their humans and prefer to be inside with them. The sensitive nature of the Dane is hurt if it is exiled to an outdoor environment and never allowed to interact with its humans in their home. Some breeders have pointed out that a Dane penned away from human companionship actually suffers from this rejection. Sometimes such a dog will strive all the more for attention and try to get inside. The drive for attention by a neglected pet can also lead to destructive behavior.

Children and Great Danes

Great Danes can be excellent companions for children. Some Danes seem to have an innate love for young humans, and other than the accidental spills that a big dog can sometimes

Children and Great Danes get along well together if both of them are well trained!

cause a small child, the two get along well together.

Children are sometimes less reliable than Great Danes about being gentle and kind. After they get over their initial awe of such a huge dog, some children cannot be trusted not to injure this biggest of dogs. Children must be reminded that this is a dog, not a pony, and the dog is not to be ridden, kicked, or struck. They must be cautioned about nose or tail pulling and eye or ear poking. Very small children or not-too-trustworthy older children should always be supervised by an adult when allowed to spend time with a Great Dane.

While Great Danes are normally very good with children, responsible parents should teach their children that a strange dog is not to be approached until an adult says it is okay to do so. Parents should also tell their children that there are times when a dog, even a Great Dane, is not in the mood to be a good play-

mate. When a dog is eating, when a female has puppies nearby, or when a dog is injured, the animal is best left alone. Overly aggressive dogs should never be allowed near children, and overly aggressive children should probably never be allowed near dogs.

Great Danes with Other Dogs

Great Danes are not usually bullies. They have no need to be. Their size alone seems to intimidate all but the feistiest dogs. While male Danes, like many males of many other breeds, are territorial as far as others of their gender are concerned, a strange dog won't have much to fear from the big dogs unless it is actually intruding on a Dane's space. A wise Dane owner, however, tries to avoid problems and always keeps a male Great Dane under firm control when there is a possibility of trouble.

Generally a Great Dane can learn to live with other dogs in a household with no more difficulty than most other breeds. Of course, bringing two strange adult unneutered males into the same household and expecting them to act like playful puppies shows little awareness of dogs and their behavior.

Giant dogs bring giant responsibilities. As with other breeds, there are aggressive, "chip-on-the-shoulder" Danes, just as there are Danes that would never attack another dog, even with provocation. By obtaining a Great Dane from bloodlines that have sound temperaments, by providing that dog with the necessary training, and by being in control of the Dane at all times when strange dogs are near, a pet owner should have few worries.

Great Danes with Other Pets

Many Great Dane breeders relate how their Danes not only get along with cats and other family pets, but actually come to be pals with the other animals. As with strange dogs and the Great Dane, a good dose of preparation laced with common sense is appropriate here. If you bring an adult Great Dane that has never been around small animals into a home setting, there may be problems. If a Dane puppy is reared with other pets, it comes to view them as part of the home, and no problems are apt to occur.

Great Danes and Strangers

Great Danes are not always fond of strangers. These dogs like to know what they will encounter in their environment. A visitor in the home who is accepted by the Dane's owners may be treated with cool reserve at first. After showing that he or she is no threat to the home or the dog's owner, the stranger may receive a variety of responses ranging from being benignly ignored to being lavishly adored. One Great Dane owner told of her daughter's boyfriend, who was met with Dane aloofness in the beginning and became a fond playmate after the dog got to know him. This Dane so liked the suitor that it would vie with the daughter for the young man's time when he visited.

Great Danes that have been thoroughly socialized as youngsters should have no trouble accepting mannerly strangers either in the home or out on a walk. The very size of the Dane should be enough to discourage strangers from bothering its owner. One Great Dane owner who lives in New York City mentioned that panhandlers always avoided him when he walked with his dog, even though the dog was extremely gentle.

Great Danes can be the gentlest of dogs, but they are still dogs; they don't always understand that a child, another animal, or a stranger means them no harm. Part of the responsibility of being a Dane owner is anticipating and eliminating situations or conditions in which the dog might feel a threat to its safety or that of its family. Because dogs may have few options in responding to a real or imagined threat, they sometimes bite. Great Danes are certainly not among the breeds that bite the most, but being a giant breed, when they do bite it is noticeable. Wise Great Dane owners protect their pets, their children, and their visitors by preventing problems before they happen!

A kennel or fenced yard designed for the average dog will not keep a giant Dane inside. Even with a good dog house with a strong and high fence, a Great Dane will want and need to be inside with the humans it adores!

25

HOW-TO:
Dane-Proofing Your Home

A potential Dane owner should be practical, as well as sympathetic to a dog's plight. By recognizing that a "great"-sized dog should in all fairness be spared the reprimands that are inevitable in a household unprepared for such a large pet, a responsible Dane owner therefore will:

• Place breakable items well above the swishing tail of a happy Dane.

• Keep all tempting morsels away from tables, countertops, and other reachable places when the Great Dane is inside or unsupervised.

• Crate train any Great Dane that lives inside and make sure that the dog has its own special place, away from the general hubbub of a household.

• Train the Dane to stay out of or off of places and furniture where the dog is not wanted.

• Alert older people and small children to the dog's inadvertent potential to cause a fall.

• Make certain that the Dane is obedient to commands and has been taught good canine manners, like not jumping up on people!

• Never forget that the Great Dane, whether puppy or adult, was invited into this home, and the humans who live there are responsible for seeing that problems are avoided, not the Dane.

This commonly used method of stopping a dog from jumping up on you doesn't work so well with a Dane that is bigger than you are! This lesson and many others are best taught when the Dane is still a puppy.

Caring for Your Great Dane

Ownership of any dog involves certain responsibilities, and giant dogs entail added responsibilities in terms of general care. Responsible Dane owners will learn what good pet care means and will do their best to see that such care is provided. Great Danes have much to offer as companion dogs, but their care is somewhat different from that needed by other dog breeds.

Housing a Giant Dog—Inside and Outside

It is understandable, indeed obvious, that the space needs of Great Danes are different from those of schnauzers, corgis, or Afghan hounds. Just what those needs are may not be as clear. It has been suggested that a prospective Dane owner take a yardstick or a measuring tape around the house and measure potential problem areas so that an adult Great Dane can be kept out of troublesome situations as much as possible. Great Dane height is but one concern; its weight and the length of its body when on all fours must also be taken into account.

A large family in a very tiny apartment probably doesn't need any dog, but it certainly does not need a Great Dane. The first rule for housing a pet is to make sure that the pet is safe. With too many human beings in a small space, a young puppy—even a young Great Dane—is in danger of being stepped on, sat on, or being pushed around and left with no specific place to call its own.

The crate: The best method of enabling a dog to live inside is to provide for it, from its very first night in the home, a cage, crate, or carrier that will be its own special place within the household (see Crate Training, page 52). The use of a crate as a home-within-the-home for a dog makes use of a natural instinct that all dogs, as denning creatures, seem to have. In the wild, canines are born in and spend a good portion of their lives in and around a lair or den that offers safety from the outside world.

By using the denning behavior of dogs to good effect, humans have been able to make dogs like the Great Dane feel safer and more comfortable within

A dog house for a Great Dane can't be a discarded crate or an old barrel. Danes need a lot of room and a draft-free, shaded dog house for the times they stay outside.

27

a house, and have also used this behavior as an aid in training (see Housebreaking, page 49). The crate will be discussed more fully in another section, but a prospective Great Dane owner should know that the process known as "crate training" is absolutely the best way to keep a Dane in the confines of a human abode!

The doghouse: Since Great Danes are often both inside and outside dogs, a dog house within a kennel run or a fenced backyard is also a good idea for this breed. Such a house should be built with the rapid growth of a Dane in mind (see page 59). This house should be constructed specifically for the needs of the Dane; it should not be just a used shipping box, old chicken coop, or discarded wooden barrel. The construction of a doghouse should take into account local climatic conditions, with the goal of providing a warm, dry, draft-free place for the dog to go when it is not with you inside your home. The illustration (see page 27). shows one type of house that has proven successful with Great Danes. The house should be protected from the sun, either by shade trees or by an awning that will prevent overheating.

The yard: The area around a Dane's outside quarters also deserves consideration. Giant dog ownership calls for giant responsibility in this area too. A backyard or kennel fence that could keep many smaller breeds securely inside is merely an easy jump for a Great Dane. Most Dane breeders believe that a fence should be at least 6 feet (180 cm) high to keep a giant, athletic dog inside it.

The construction of the fence is also important. Danes are, as mentioned, "leaners." If a 150 pound (68 kg) dog leans on a poorly constructed fence, door, or gate long enough, it can fall. Some Danes are great diggers and can squeeze their big bodies *under* some fences that they can't go over.

It is also important that the Dane's outside area be free from unsafe obstacles that could hurt the dog. A good Dane owner will make a safety survey of the area accessible to the dog to identify and eliminate places or conditions of potential danger.

Tip: The use of the yardstick outside may be helpful in determining what is in reach of an inquisitive Dane.

Exercise and the Great Dane

Great Danes, although very big, athletic dogs, are calmer than some other breeds. While a Dane that lives primarily inside needs adequate exercise to stay healthy, it is also true that an outside dog may not get all the physical activity that it needs for good health just by being in a run or small backyard.

Daily exercise to keep pets in good physical and mental shape can take the form of regular walks with their owners or other members of their families. The Dane and the human will benefit from being together for a special time on a consistent basis, and at the same time they will enjoy all the cardiovascular benefits of steady strolling.

Giant dogs create a need for extra awareness even when out on a walk. If the Great Dane weighs 150 pounds (68 kg) and the human weighs less than 100 pounds (45 kg), control of the dog must rest on more than physical domination. An out-of-control Chihuahua can be scooped up into the arms of its owner and thus rescued from a harmful situation. Not many people are able to handle a Great Dane in the same way. While the chapter on training (see Training Your Great Dane, page 48) deals more thoroughly with overall basic training, some suggestions on how to walk safely with a dog that is bigger than you follow here:

Start early: Begin walking a Dane when it is still a puppy and you are bigger than it is. A puppy that learns to "heel" and respond to the "heel" command while young is much more controllable as an adult.

Be consistent in what you allow the dog, especially a young dog, to do and see that each family member exercises the dog in the same way. Don't allow "No" to mean "No" today and "Maybe" tomorrow. If a puppy doesn't get the same response from its human companion each time it tests the limits, it will become confused and be likely to ignore other commands.

Pay attention: Be alert to potentially dangerous situations. If your young dog is going to act up, it will rarely do so when you are alone with it in the safety of your backyard. Impulsive puppy behavior can occur in the middle of a crosswalk on a busy street or when you are occupied with something or someone else. It only takes a moment of inattention for a dog to pull the leash out of your hand and run under the wheels of an oncoming car.

Buy and keep good equipment for exercising your pet. Make sure that collars fit correctly and are in good shape, not likely to break at the pull of an anxious or enthusiastic big dog. Take the same care with leashes, watching for signs of wear and for broken or worn-out snaps or clasps.

Have fun: Make walks enjoyable times for you and the dog. Don't yield to the negative attitude that walking the dog is a loathsome chore. Walking with you will be one of the high points of your Great Dane's day, and if the dog picks up negative vibes from you, its pleasure in the outing can be diminished.

Grooming Your Great Dane

A Great Dane is a good deal easier to groom than many other breeds. Although there is much more surface

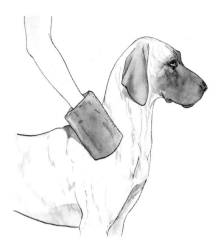

Grooming your Great Dane, with its short coat, isn't as difficult as it is with some breeds, but don't neglect grooming. Your Dane will look and feel better if you pay attention to its appearance.

area on a Great Dane, keeping the big dog clean and presentable is not a huge task. The following pointers can make that task easier to master:

The dog's face: Because the Dane's face is so important a part of the beauty of the animal, make every effort to keep the ears, eyes, muzzle, and chin clean. These areas are difficult for your dog to clean by itself.

Baths: Don't bathe your Dane too often, and when you do be sure to use products made specifically for pets. Too-frequent shampooing will make the Dane's coat and skin dry and possibly flaky. If a house dog gets really dirty, then a bath is necessary.

Teeth: Clean your Dane's teeth. This grooming task is best started while the dog is a puppy. Your veterinarian can show you how.

Feet and nails: Feet and toenails need regular inspection. From puppyhood on, it is very important to keep a Great Dane's nails evenly trimmed to avoid foot problems, which can be aggravated by the large size and weight of the Dane (see Toenails, page 80).

Parasites: Watch for external parasites. Fleas, ticks, and ear mites can make your Great Dane (and you) miserable and spread diseases. Keep

This blue Dane watches over a blue puppy.

these critters away from your pet (see Parasites, page 72).

Boarding Your Great Dane

Boarding your Great Dane is a plausible alternative to the rigors and stresses of extended travel. There are several options for boarding your dog:
• There are many quality boarding kennels across the country that are accredited with the American

Great Danes need regular exercise every day to stay in good shape.

Boarding Kennel Association (ABKA) (see Useful Addresses and Literature, page 92); The ABKA teaches its member kennels the best ways to care for their clients' pets. Some boarding kennel owners will possess the coveted CKO (Certified Kennel Operator) designation showing that they have studied their craft and passed numerous tests.
• Your Great Dane may be able to stay at home under the care of family, friends, or neighbors.
• Professional pet sitters also enable your dog to stay in its own home. Pet sitters should have references and be bonded.
• Your veterinarian may have space to board your dog at his or her clinic.
• Under certain circumstances, if your Dane's breeder lives nearby, he or she might allow the dog to visit for a few days.

Providing Tangibles and Intangibles

Caring for your Great Dane should never be allowed to become a hard or unpleasant task. Your Dane depends on you for almost everything that affects its life. When you become a dog owner, especially the owner of a dog with the special needs of the Great Dane, you have a responsibility to the animal.

You must provide many tangible benefits: housing, food and water, medical care. These tangibles are identified and known before you get a dog, and they are an essential part of keeping a pet.

There are some intangible things that your Great Dane deserves also: your attention, your correction, your affection. Unless you provide these intangibles, your Great Dane becomes merely a big, living possession. Unless you truly care for the Dane, the value of the care you give in tangible ways is diminished. There is nothing worse than a Great Dane banished from the

Whenever your Dane is away from home, you should be in complete control of your pet at all times.

household because it grew "too big" and relegated to a lonely and frustrating life in a kennel, seeing its humans only when they bring the perfunctory food and water. Some might say that in such circumstances a Great Dane should be euthanized, or certainly taken away from you and placed in the hands of owners who will let the dog express its love and receive their love in return.

A Great Dane puppy in your care can become a wonderful pet and companion. It can be a part of your life, anticipating your highs and lows and trying its canine best to share them with you. It can be a watchdog, a nursemaid, a friend, and a noninterrupting listener, but it has to be molded into a great pet and companion. Such a dog will not develop by accident, and it will not be developed by a person who doesn't care deeply *for* the dog, as well as take proper care *of* the dog.

Great Danes and their owners will benefit from regular walks every day.

HOW-TO:
Traveling with Your Great Dane

Traveling with your Great Dane can be a good experience, but the dog's size makes some forms of travel less practical than with smaller dogs. When contemplating taking your Dane on a trip, try to visualize the experience from two perspectives:

1. Will my Great Dane be safe on this trip?

2. Will my Great Dane be comfortable on this trip?

Your dog should always be in its carrier when riding in your automobile. Large dogs require large carriers, however, and the automobile may not accommodate a large crate. *Never* let your dog, even on short trips, ride outside the carrier in the car. It might seem pleasant to have your big dog peering over your shoulder, but in the event of a sudden stop the Dane can be sent crashing against the car's interior or even into you. It is easy for a dog, even a giant, sturdy Great Dane, to be injured or to become a missile that can carom inside the car. Letting your dog ride outside its crate in the back of an open pickup truck is never wise. In car or truck, use the crate for safety!

Safety tip: Never leave a Great Dane in a parked car, even with the windows rolled down. The dog can be killed by heatstroke in only a few minutes (see Heatstroke, page 77), even when the outside temperature is only as high as 60°F (16°C). When you travel by car with your Dane (safe in its carrier), always concern yourself with the animal's needs. You can do several things to make motoring a more pleasant experience for everyone in the car:

• Don't feed your Dane four to six hours prior to leaving.

• Don't give it water less than two hours prior to leaving.

• Check with your veterinarian about the advisability of motion-sickness medication for your dog.

• Try to stop every hour to give the dog a respite from the confines of the carrier, a relief break, and a brief drink of water. Always use a collar and leash when your dog is out of its carrier.

• When using interstate rest areas, walk your dog in designated "pet walk" places and pay close attention to your dog while it is at the rest area. There are many sources of harm in public places: antifreeze spills, broken glass, or inattentive drivers, for example.

• If you and your pet are going to stay in a motel or hotel on your trip, call ahead and find a place that will allow a well-mannered pet to stay in the room with its owner. Never try to slip your Dane into a hotel where pets are not allowed. This is not only rude behavior, but also a crime in some places!

• Unless you are certain that the place you are visiting has the same dog food your dog eats, take enough with you.

• Before going across state lines or international boundaries, be sure your Dane has all the required shots and a health

certificate from your veterinarian attesting to this fact.

Air Travel

Traveling by plane with your Great Dane isn't exactly the same as for the owner of a Yorkshire terrier or other toy breed that can sometimes accompany its owner in its carrier, of course. Unless it is absolutely essential that you fly with your Great Dane, leaving the dog at home would be a better option.

If your Dane must go airborne, here are some guidelines to follow:

• If your dog's cage, crate, or carrier is not an approved airline model, you may be able to rent one from the airline.

• Have your veterinarian give your Great Dane a physical and provide you with a health certificate, which is now a mandatory requirement on all airlines. This certificate cannot be dated more than 10 days prior to your departure date.

• Fly on the same plane as your pet. Avoid rerouting problems by getting direct flights and traveling from hub airports. Some airlines charge much more if your pet has to change planes. When you make your airline reservations, fully discuss your travel plans, including arrangements for your Dane, with the airline personnel.

• *Be early* for all flights; airlines often require that animal passengers be checked in two hours before flight time.

• Be sure your carrier is in good shape and its door and latch are in good working order.

• Other than the carrier conversion kit, don't put any food or water in the carrier. That would only create a mess.

• Discuss the use of canine tranquilizers with your veterinarian.

• Insist on seeing your dog loaded onto the airplane. Be polite but assertive with airline personnel. Impress upon them the value of your Great Dane to you and the lengths to which you will go to ensure its safety and comfort.

• Always discuss with your veterinarian the advisability of your dog's making this trip. Very old and very young dogs might be better left at home (see Boarding Your Great Dane, page 30).

Considerations Before You Buy a Great Dane

Ownership of a Great Dane isn't really like ownership of a smaller dog. That the Dane requires more room is clear. That a giant dog may have greater needs than ample living space may not be as obvious.

Illusion and Reality

There are many things about this breed that can make a Great Dane a truly special pet, given the right home. Some aspects of Dane ownership may be incompatible with your household

Great Danes are adorable as puppies. Some people aren't prepared for the Dane to grow up, and the innocent dog ends up at an animal shelter. The Dane will need good care and good training from puppy-hood on if it is to be a good pet as an adult.

routine. Deciding whether this breed fits your needs, wishes, and expectations is a task that no Great Dane breeder, no dog authority, and no book can perform for you. The decision must be made by you and the other members of your family. Failure to take this decision seriously may result in inconvenience for the humans and tragedy for the dog.

Sad to say, the Great Dane often suffers when it fails to live up to the owner's fantasy. Some people buy a Great Dane in order to have the biggest, meanest dog in the neighborhood. Others imagine themselves strolling in the park with a magnificent Dane drawing the admiration and envy of passersby. Still others envision themselves lounging in their book-lined den with a giant canine companion stretched out at their feet. Strangely, some people who have never exhibited a dog of any breed in a dog show see themselves obtaining a Great Dane so splendid that everyone at its very first show is in absolute awe of the dog and its novice owner.

These mental gymnastics are effortless; the realization of these dreams is quite another matter. A person should rethink the decision to get a Dane in order to have "the biggest, toughest dog in town." The Great Dane can certainly fill the size requirement and some Danes could conceivably become dominant and aggressive, but such behavior runs counter to what a well-bred Dane should be (see AKC standard, page 15). Forcing a dog into a pattern that is alien or contrary to its genetic make-up is true cruelty to the animal.

A Great Dane owner can surely look forward to sharing peaceful moments at home. The Dane does have a reasonably low activity level and can be an excellent home companion, but not without adequate preparation and training. Developing a Great Dane into an acceptable member of a household requires caring, knowledgeable, consistent help from the humans in that household. That process takes time and effort.

Exhibiting Danes or any other breed is a difficult skill, and it may take years to master. Showing your Great Dane may be an excellent interest to pursue, but to achieve success with your first dog or even your fifth may require the expertise of a professional handler. To succeed early on you must obtain the right Great Dane, listen to the right breeders, judges, and handlers, follow all the right suggestions, and have the right amount of luck.

Remember that, first and foremost, a good Great Dane should be a good pet. It should be temperamentally compatible with you and your family, able to adjust to your family circumstances, and capable of the things you realistically want a pet dog to be or do. One of the most rewarding aspects of dog ownership is taking a young, impressionable pup and shaping it into a truly excellent adult dog.

Searching for the Right Dog

Having decided that you and the Great Dane are right for each other, you next have to find exactly the right Dane for you. This process may take time and effort. While Great Danes are not rare, the dog or puppy with the right temperament, health history, potential, color, sex, age, and other particulars may not be easy to locate.

Where to Look

If you have been studying the breed at dog shows, you may already know Great Dane breeders in your area. They are an excellent place to begin your quest. Talk with several of these Dane breeders or exhibitors, ask questions, and take notes. Get their recommendations of possible sources.

There may be a Great Dane breeders organization in your city or state. After you have presented yourself as a serious and well-prepared potential Dane owner, most of these breeders should be willing to help you find a dog. In fact, these organizations may be the only way to find exactly what you want. Great Dane breeder/exhibitors generally know who among their peers has a litter of pups, an older pet-quality puppy, or an adult Dane in need of a good home. Because these are the people who show dogs, they probably can help you find a pup with dog show potential.

If you have trouble finding a local Great Dane club, contact the national club (see page 92) or the American Kennel Club (see page 92) for information about well-known Great Dane enthusiasts not far away from you. The American Kennel Club also has an excellent video about Great Danes. This videotape would probably be a very good investment for any potential Dane owner.

There are specialized magazines available that deal with Great Danes (see page 92). By learning as much as you can about Dane breeders, you will be in a better position to choose the place to obtain your Dane.

Clarifying Your Objectives

In your search for a Great Dane, you must clarify your objectives. Just what do you want this dog to do for you? If you are looking for a show dog, go to dog shows and talk with the top breeders of Great Danes. If you want a good companion and pet, talk to the dog

Finding the just-right Great Dane puppy will be an interesting and very important task.

show people and let them know of your interest in a pet-quality puppy. If you have decided that a fawn Great Dane is the color you like best, by all means seek a good fawn. There should be enough available for you to get a fawn dog at the quality level you want.

You must decide what criteria you have for the dog, but above all else, the Dane should be a good pet and companion for you and your family. Good temperament and good health are more important than show quality or colors. The finest show winner in the world is no bargain if it has an unsound temperament.

What Should Be Expected of You

Great Dane breeders will be more than willing to help a newcomer find a good dog or puppy, but they are serious about their hobby and will also expect some things of you. They want evidence that you are serious about owning a Great Dane and intend to give a Dane the best possible home.

Breeders want to know what kind of environment you will provide for your Great Dane. They may also want to know about your experience with other dogs. Is this Dane to be your first dog? You may want to take good care of a Great Dane, but do you know how to do so?

Some breeders will question your reasons for wanting a Great Dane. Do you want a big, handsome dog to serve as a fashion accessory? Do you want an attack dog? Do you want a Dane because your neighbors got a big dog and you want a bigger one?

If you want a show-quality Great Dane puppy, many breeders ask if you are willing—or will allow the breeder—to put forth the time, effort, and money to campaign this dog to affirm its championship potential. What if the dog doesn't win? Do you plan on having your pet spayed or neutered? Be prepared for this type of quizzing, and remember that Dane enthusiasts want to make certain that their puppies go to loving homes.

What You Should Expect

When you approach a Great Dane breeder about a puppy or an older dog, you should expect honest answers from a knowledgeable source. Try to approach someone known not only for producing good-quality Great Danes, but also for possessing a good personal reputation.

You should generally expect to pay several hundred dollars for a pet and perhaps several thousand for a top show prospect. Beware of bargains. The dog-owning world is full of people who, to save money, took a lesser-quality puppy than they wanted. Some Dane buyers choose to buy their pups from sources other than reputable breeders and soon discover that the bargain puppy becomes the most expensive pet they have ever owned.

In a breed where the potential for health problems is admittedly higher than in some others, you *must* seek out the best-quality Great Dane possible. Newspaper ads and other sources may advertise a Dane puppy "with all the papers." One well-known breeder who bought her first Dane from such a source stated, "I discovered that the only papers I actually ever saw for this puppy were the ones on the floor of the room it was in." Your Great Dane is not only a financial investment, but also a canine friend who will share your home and life for perhaps a decade or more. Can you afford to buy a close-companion animal without having as much documentation and information as possible?

Before selecting a puppy from a source, make certain that the Dane has these vital documents and necessary records:

Health records: Current health records showing the dates of all vaccinations, wormings, and examinations by a licensed veterinarian, including the results and treatments.

Pedigree: An accurate pedigree showing the puppy's parentage. The Great Dane Club of America has strong recommendations suggesting what colors of Danes should be mated together. Your potential pup's pedigree should show that these color-breeding recommendations have been followed. The pedigree should also show the champions or obedience title holders in your prospective pup's ancestry.

AKC registration: The AKC (American Kennel Club) registration certificate, which confirms that the Great Dane puppy is purebred, with its mother (dam) and father (sire) both being registered Great Danes. You should also receive application forms to forward to the AKC in order to register this puppy, if you buy it, in your name.

You may find an older Dane that, with awareness and patience on your part, could be a wonderful pet.

HD screening: You will want documented evidence that the parents of this puppy have tested free of signs of HD (Hip Dysplasia, see page 71). While this does not ensure that their offspring will not become dysplastic, the tests, which are performed after a dog is two years old, are the best screening technique for this malady currently available.

If you can't get the papers listed above, do not buy the puppy. Don't accept the puppy on the proviso that "the papers are in the mail." Most Dane breeders are honest, but this is a very important purchase. Good business practices on your part are only wise.

Most of all you should expect that your study and careful search for a Great Dane will result in a healthy, temperamentally sound puppy with no genetic defects or inherited physical problems. Your entire experience as a novice Great Dane owner will be affected by your ability to be a knowledgeable, assertive, and careful consumer.

Guarantees—from Both Sides

Most responsible Great Dane breeders will give you a written health and temperament guarantee for any puppy they sell. It should specify that the dog's inherited health and temperament are guaranteed for the life of the animal. Breeders who are that confident of the quality of their dogs are the best sources for your Great Dane puppy.

Reputable breeders usually have some requirements for you as well. Since many Great Dane breeders take the dogs they sell as lifelong responsibilities, they may have some agreements for you to sign:

Spaying or neutering: One such agreement involves your commitment to have spayed or neutered a pet-quality dog or puppy, in order to keep an inferior show specimen from producing inferior puppies. This does not imply that the dog or puppy has physi-

cal or temperamental shortcomings, merely that its color may not be just right or that some other minor cosmetic flaw is in evidence. Some breeders make a practice of withholding the registration papers until the dog or puppy buyer brings proof from a veterinarian that the animal has been spayed or neutered.

Returning the puppy: Other Great Dane breeders want to be certain you know that they maintain a strong proprietorial interest in the Dane you are buying. If you cannot keep the dog or puppy, the breeder will probably want you to agree to return it rather than pass the animal on to someone else or to the humane society. This for-life concern is another sign that you have come to a good breeder.

A Puppy or an Older Dog?

The choice here is largely determined by what you want in a Great Dane. If you have had considerable success as a dog owner and merely want a companion, there may be an adult Great Dane, perhaps from a rescue group or even an animal shelter, that could move right in and become your best friend. Some adults and older puppies just don't work out with their initial buyers. In other cases, circumstances may necessitate the return of the Dane to the breeder. Quite often these Great Danes can adapt readily to your home, and in a short time it will seem that they have been around forever. Other dogs, however, have picked up bad habits or made attachments to their former owners that may be hard to break.

If you take your time in the choice of an adult Great Dane, you may find the perfect dog for you and your family. You may be able to help retrain or readapt a maladjusted adult, although that may not have been your original purpose. If you can get the sound, healthy pet you want *and* help an adult Great Dane in need of a good home, then you and the dog are indeed fortunate.

Puppies require a lot of time and effort to become the kind of pet you are seeking. A novice dog owner should probably choose a puppy and let the youngster grow up with the family as the family learns how to train and care for the pet. As adaptable as some older Danes can be, a puppy learns the lessons it is taught usually for the very first time. No retraining or restructuring is required with a youngster, which will know only what you teach it.

Whether you choose a puppy or an adult, take equal care. Your main goal is ownership of a good pet. Both adult and puppy Danes can fit this description, but each presents either a set of behaviors to change or a set of behaviors to develop. You have to decide which task best suits you and your family.

A Male or a Female?

Your expectations will also influence your decision about the gender of your pet. Male Great Danes are usually larger than females; they possess a bearing and presence seen in males of many breeds, but especially marked in Great Danes. Males are more territorial than females, and perhaps more likely to attempt escape from the backyard in order to "cruise" the neighborhood.

Although they tower over males and females of most other breeds, female Great Danes should be decidedly feminine in their graceful, elegant appearance. They are somewhat less aloof with strangers and other dogs than are males. Unspayed females go into heat with the estrous cycle about every six months and must be strictly safeguarded at these times to prevent unwanted litters.

A properly trained, well-bred Great Dane of either sex should be an excellent pet. Unless you have serious aspirations as a Great Dane breeder and unless a Dane is of exceptional quality and worthy of being used for breeding, your pet should be spayed or neutered. The females will not have estrous cycles and will remain the same vibrant pets. The males will lose none of their powerful, regal nature but will be less likely to become overly aggressive or overly adventuresome. Most owners of spayed or neutered pets notice only that their dogs are a bit more attentive to their humans. Other than the need to watch your dog's diet to avoid obesity, the negatives of spaying and neutering are negligible. Spaying or neutering can also help your Dane avoid other

When picking up a gangly Dane pup, always support the pup's rear end with one hand while holding it comfortably under the chest with the other hand.

With the right amount of love, care, and training, this little brindle pup could become a great Great Dane.

puppy as a stud fee payment. The youngster progressed well until the breeder noticed a possibly heritable fault, and that ended the show and breeding career of this Great Dane. The once top-pick puppy became a lovely spayed pet for a family that adores her.

Because truly great show dogs are rare in any breed, a puppy with show potential is significantly more expensive than a puppy already identified as a pet prospect. Furthermore, as a novice in Great Danes and in the show ring, you have little chance of being allowed to buy a top-flight show-potential puppy unless you agree to provide the puppy with every chance to achieve its show ring potential. Ads for show dogs often read "Show homes only."

If you believe that exhibiting dogs is for you, one approach is to own a promising pup in partnership with a breeder. The dog may stay with the breeder or handler for a portion of each year, but you and your family will have an opportunity to see your dog competing against other quality Great Danes. If that sounds good to you and your family, the investment in a show prospect puppy may be well worth it.

health problems, like mammary or prostate cancer.

Pet Quality or Show Quality?

A pet-quality Great Dane is not less healthy, less temperamentally sound, or—other than cosmetically—less a Great Dane than a show-quality dog. Conversely, a show-quality Dane should not sacrifice health or temperament to be a show dog. Both categories of Great Danes should be excellent companion animals. Without that capacity, you don't really want either of them!

If the show ring is your goal, your best bet is to buy a puppy with "show potential." In the experienced eye of a Great Dane breeder, a puppy with such potential looks like other puppies that later became successful show dogs.

Puppies change a great deal as they mature. Although many show-potential puppies live up to a breeder's expectations, others don't, and they are reassigned to the pet-quality ranks. In a common practice, one Dane breeder took back a pick-of-litter

Choosing a Great Dane Puppy

By this time you and your family have decided what you want in a Great Dane puppy. You have given the matter considerable thought and study. You have assessed your household's capacity to provide a good home for a Great Dane. You have visited a number of dog shows and seen what really good Great Danes look like. You have talked with, perhaps even visited with, Dane breeders and seen their dogs and their homes. You have puppy-proofed your home and had a high fence erected around the backyard. You now seem ready to choose a puppy.

Several breeders near your home have litters of pups in the color you like. You have decided that a healthy, pet-quality female puppy with a good disposition is what you want. You recognize that there is enough demand, even for the pet pups, that the price may be several hundred dollars.

When you visit these breeders, ask to look only at the female pet prospects. This simplifies your choice, and you won't become attracted to a show-potential pup, only to be told that it doesn't fit your pup-profile. Take time to observe the puppies; watch them interact with each other and with their mother. Carefully handle each puppy, paying attention to the ones that seem alert, unafraid, and well adjusted. After you have carefully looked at each pup, ask the breeder about the puppy you like best.

If you get sidetracked and become interested in a puppy that doesn't fit your pup-profile, you should probably reassess the profile. Commit to buying a puppy only after *your* veterinarian has examined it and found it healthy and free from serious defects, including temperament. Then, and only then, have you found your new canine family member.

How to lift a puppy correctly: Even as youngsters, Great Danes are not exactly small. When picking up a gangly, full-of-fun Dane puppy, always support its rear end with one hand. Hold the youngster comfortably under the chest with your other hand. In this way, you can look at a puppy without danger of it jumping or falling from your grasp.

Christmas Puppies

Contrary to the various advertisements that show the joy on a child's face when it gets a pup for Christmas, Christmas puppies are *not* a good idea. Bringing a new puppy into the happy chaos of Christmas morning is both unfair and unwise. The puppy

has probably never been away from its mother and littermates before, and it suddenly finds itself in the midst of people shouting with glee, tearing open packages, and concerned with just about everything except the well-being of a frightened or bewildered young Great Dane.

Your new family member deserves to be the center of attention, to have its needs met, to be helped in adjusting to this strange new world. Unless the puppy is the *only* gift your family exchanges this holiday, let the puppy come well before or well after Christmas.

One idea with real merit is to buy the AKC videotape about Great Danes and books about the breed and wrap these as gifts to put under the tree. Then you have given the family not only something to build anticipation, but also good information that will prove useful later.

A well-bred, well-groomed, and well-handled Great Dane at a dog show is something to remember.

HOW-TO:
Is the Great Dane Right for You?

Acquiring a Great Dane: You cannot find the right Dane pup without spending an appropriate amount of time deciding just what you want. Are you prepared to study the breed, then invest money and effort in visiting dog shows and Dane breeders?

Training: Are you prepared to train and socialize a Great Dane? Danes can be stubborn and willful if they are not properly socialized and adequately trained. A small dog that wants everything its own way is bad enough, but imagine a Dane that wants to be boss! *No one should own an untrained Dane!*

Puppy Proofing: An active, inquisitive puppy that will soon stand a yard high can make a mess of a house that hasn't been prepared. Are you pre-

pared to puppy-proof *before* the puppy comes home? Remember that Great Danes, for all their attributes and potential, are still dogs, and giant dogs at that. All the trouble that an average-sized dog can get into is multiplied when you consider a Great Dane. You must plan ahead. For example, a 4 foot (120 cm) high fence that would safely contain a bulldog or a chow-chow isn't going to keep a Great Dane at home.

Great Danes need great owners if they are to be the best possible pet they can be. Pet ownership involves not just loving an animal, but providing training and correction when needed, even when the dog weighs as much as you do!

HOW-TO:
Are You Right for the Great Dane?

Now, if you have taken a hard look at the Great Dane in the clear light of reality to decide whether such a dog, with its pluses and minuses, is the dog for you, you must proceed to scrutinize the other side of the equation with equal diligence. If you are wrong about whether the Dane is right for you, perhaps you can make some adjustments to improve things; if you are wrong about whether *you* are right for the Dane, what can the unfortunate dog do?

Answer candidly the following questions and any others that can help you know for sure:

• Is owning a Great Dane an idea that has been carefully considered, or is it an impulsive wish?

• Does each member of your family understand what responsibilities owning a Great Dane will entail?

• Is each member of your family willing to accept these responsibilities and the work and care involved?

• Is your family financially able to give a giant dog the space (a yard or outside kennel with a high fence), food, medical care, and other tangible and intangible things it may need?

• Do you have the willpower to resist the impulse to purchase a puppy because you feel sorry for it or because it is a bargain?

• Will you be able to resist a readily available or attractively priced puppy to get precisely the Dane you want?

• Have you and your family discussed in realistic terms the relatively short life span of Great Danes as a breed and how this may affect your ownership of a Great Dane?

• Have you studied Great Danes and decided which color, sex, age, and background might be right for you?

If each family member can honestly answer these questions in the affirmative, then you have done part of your homework to prepare for owning a Great Dane. The next step is to begin your search for the right Dane to join your family.

Bringing Your Great Dane Home

Before you bring your Great Dane home, take some steps to ensure the dog's comfort and safety. Of course, the first step in this process began when you carefully considered whether you and this dog were right for each other. Because you felt, after much thought, that a Dane would fit your needs for a dog and you would fit the Dane's needs for an owner, you have arrived at this point—bringing your new pet home.

The Initial Phases

If you have visited your puppy several times at the breeder's, you have already begun the bonding process that will make you and your pet a team. The bonding process with your

Danes don't stay small for long. Their owners need to plan ahead for the time when little pups become giant dogs.

dog, in combination with early socialization with other humans, cannot be overestimated in its significance in helping your puppy grow to be the best-adjusted adult possible. Remember that being well adjusted takes on added importance when a dog is as large as a Great Dane.

Your pup's breeder will know the best time for the youngster to leave the only home it has ever known and go home with you. Departure is always stressful to a puppy, especially a puppy of a sensitive breed like the Great Dane. As the caring owner of a bewildered puppy, you will want to make this adjustment as easy to accomplish as possible.

Introductory period: Getting to know your new puppy while it is still at the breeder's is usually a good idea. If a few brief visits and some playtime with the puppy without its dam or siblings present are geographically convenient and in keeping with the breeder's wishes, your Dane will be leaving home with friends instead of strangers. This introductory period may not be necessary or possible with every pup, but if the opportunity to ease yourself and your family into the young dog's life presents itself, by all means take it.

The trip home: Although the use of a cage, crate, or carrier is always recommended when transporting a canine by automobile, this first trip home is an exception. Let a responsible person hold the puppy in his or her arms, but be sure that the puppy holder has protective clothing and a couple of old towels handy in case the pup suffers from motion sickness.

If your trip home with the puppy is a long one, plan rest and relief breaks at least once each hour. Even though your Dane is still a relatively small puppy, you *must* be sure that you have a collar and leash on the dog whenever it is out of the car. A puppy can get into harm's way before most humans can react. Prevention, in the form of a good collar and leash and an alert attitude, could save your new pet's life even before it gets to its new home.

Early training: When you arrive, even before you take the puppy inside, take it *immediately* to a preselected urination and defecation spot. You may want to "salt the mine" by dropping some litter from the puppy's first home with the scent of urine or feces on it. That will encourage the pup to learn that the site is where such activities are to be done. Remember that this first relief time is very important. Stay there with the pup until it relieves itself, then enthusiastically praise it for doing the right thing at the right place at the right time. Then you can go inside and introduce the pup to your home.

Puppy-proofing measures: You most certainly should have puppy-proofed the areas to which the youngster will have access. Puppy-proofing means that you have removed from these places everything that could harm an innocent, ignorant, and inquisitive puppy. Some of these things are:
• Tight squeezes—behind a stove or upright piano or between banister railings, for example—where a puppy could get trapped or caught.
• Heavy items on tables that could tip over or fall on the puppy.
• Stairwells, patios, porches, and open windows that could lead to a fall.

• Access to common household items, like household cleaners, air fresheners, poisonous houseplants, antifreeze, exposed wiring, or extension cords, which could kill your dog if ingested or chewed.
• Small, easy-to-swallow things that could harm your pet, like tacks, pins, rubber erasers, and children's toys.
• Doors and gates to the outside that a quick puppy could dart through or get caught behind and injured.

These are just a few of the things and situations you need to eliminate or barricade for the safety of your puppy. If your puppy has access to a garage or driveway, every family member needs to be certain that the young dog is absolutely safe (on a leash with another person or in its carrier or kennel) *before* a car is moved.

Before you bring a puppy home, be sure the home is ready for the puppy and for the dog it will soon become.

45

Many pets are killed or injured by autos driven by their owners.

Great Danes grow rapidly. The tabletop that was secure from a curious Dane puppy two months ago may be within reach now. Do a complete puppy-proofing job the first time, and update your efforts every week or so as the young giant matures.

Adjustment Time

When your puppy first comes to your home, its new home, it needs time to adjust. You should be prepared to give it the affection, caring, and early lessons that will help it quickly fit into the household. A responsible person, probably an adult or an older teenager, should take several days or a long weekend to help the pup understand what is happening in its young life. Wait before inviting friends and neighbors in to see the new pup. Much of what the puppy encounters is mystifying and bewildering. If not given attention and gentle correction now, the puppy could develop bad habits that will be difficult to break. It is easier to instill the right habits initially. Until the recent memories of its old family, its mother and littermates, begin to fade, the pup needs support from its new family.

Your Dog's Den—a Plus and a Must

All dogs—from wild canines to your new puppy—prefer to have a safe haven for rest and retreat when things get stressful. The den or lair that is the birthplace of most wild canines has been suitably replaced by a carrier, cage, or crate for many house dogs.

This manufactured den will give your puppy a home-within-the-home, a unique place that is the dog's refuge, sleeping quarters, and sometimes mobile transport to the veterinarian and on trips. Use of such a man-made den will greatly aid you in helping your

puppy settle in, and it will also be an invaluable help in housebreaking the puppy (see Housebreaking, page 49).

Some humans may view a carrier as a little prison for detaining the puppy, but dogs see their dens as an area where they can relax or go when tired or bewildered. Don't let mistaken human views about the carrier cause you and your Dane to miss the benefits of instinctive denning behavior (see Crate Training Suggestions, page 52).

Helping Your Puppy Settle In

As a puppy, your Great Dane is at its learning peak. The lessons it is taught now, the impressions it gets now, can stay with the dog for the rest of its life. It is your role as human leader and puppy owner to see that your pup gets the right lessons and the right impressions. In the absence of your guidance, a puppy may not learn what it is supposed to do and what it is allowed to do.

By using the crate as a sleeping place and a spot to be when not with you, the puppy has acquired a haven to run to if it gets tired of playing or if it feels unsure or afraid. Your puppy will now have to adjust to being without its mother or litter mates.

It may seem cute to let a young puppy sleep with you, but how cute will the arrangement be with a 150 pound (68 kg) adult dog! Let the puppy sleep in its carrier. You'll be happier, and so will the dog.

Now the family must pull together and do what is best for the puppy. Beginning with the first night in the new home, no matter how much pitiful puppy-wailing or how much human hand-wringing there may be, the puppy sleeps in its carrier, *period!* Everyone in the family needs to know that this is best for the puppy. Like an inoculation, it may appear to hurt, but it is much better for the

Simple Aids to Ease Adjustment

You can help make the puppy's settling-in ordeal easier:

• Place an old-fashioned hot water bottle (the rubber kind, with no leaks to mess up the pup's quarters) in the crate. This will give the pup a sense of warmth reminiscent of its mother.

• Provide the puppy with something from its first home that has retained comforting scents.

• Wrap an old wind-up alarm clock in a towel. The ticking simulates the beating of the mother's heart. Be sure the alarm is deactivated.

• One of the more unusual ways to comfort a puppy is to place a radio near (not in) the carrier and turn it on low volume to an all-night talk radio station, which gives the puppy some sense of not being alone.

• Other aids include feeding the puppy the same food it was eating before it came to you (see Feeding Your Great Dane, page 63). Changing foods adds to the stress of its move to a new home. It is also a good idea to feed the puppy on the same schedule used at the breeder's. Regulating the puppy's mealtimes is also a good way to predict its need to go outside.

Dane in the long run. Let the puppy sleep in its carrier, initially in your room, where a firm "No" is the appropriate response to crying or whimpering yet lets the pup know you are nearby. Later, after the puppy has adjusted to the carrier and the sleeping arrangements, a different location for this haven can be found.

When the puppy is placed in the carrier for the first night it will naturally be lonely, a little frightened, and anxious to have its new humans come and comfort it. Don't do it, and don't allow anyone else in the family to do it! No matter how much you paid for this puppy, a weak moment now could turn a potentially excellent companion into a neurotic, believing that when it wants attention all it has to do is whimper and cry. This is not a good lesson for your dog to learn, and it may be very hard to unteach!

No one enjoys the prospect of a lonely puppy whimpering itself to sleep for the first few nights in its new home, but unless you want that whimpering to become a reinforced behavior, you must be firm. The puppy must learn that there is a time for interaction with its family and a time for quiet and sleep. A sad, lonely, crying puppy can become a sad, lonely, crying adult if someone in your household gives in and takes the puppy out of its special sleeping place to cuddle it every time it cries. Steel your resolve and that of your family with the knowledge that your puppy, unless wrongfully reinforced, will not continue to cry much beyond the first few days. Consistency now will be a great aid in helping the puppy reach its potential as a good family companion.

Don't let your new Great Dane puppy overexert itself. Playing with the pup is fine, but a very young puppy can only play hard in short spurts. When the puppy appears to be tiring, take it to the carrier for a little rest. This reinforces the idea of what the pup should do in its den.

Remember that this Great Dane is a puppy. Don't expect anything but puppy behavior. These initial days are for first lessons, adjustment, and settling in. If you take things slowly with the pup now, you'll have a stable foundation on which to build the other training that will come in a few months.

Training Your Great Dane

Don't Own an Untrained Dane

It is foolish to own an untrained dog of any breed, but it is the height of folly to possess a dog that you could not possibly restrain physically in numerous emergency situations. A Great Dane, which someday will weigh as much as or more than its owner, must be under the control of a human in every possible circumstance. Some control measures are high fences, stout kennels, and strong leashes attached to strong collars, but the best control of all is adequate training.

Your Great Dane may be a wonderful companion, a member of your family, and a real canine friend and protector, but the best Dane in the world is still a dog. A bitch in season in the neighborhood can turn the calmest Great Dane into a hormonally charged Romeo. If your dog will not obey your call to come to you at a time like this, then it is not fully trained and could present a danger to itself or others.

Training your Great Dane teaches the dog restraint, ingrained habits, and other specific behaviors that you can control. Without this control you have a giant problem animal that could easily get into serious trouble. Protect yourself and protect your dog; *train it!*

Using Pack Behavior to Simplify Training

Your Great Dane is a pack animal. In the days when the Dane went by the name alaunt or boarhound, the breed was often kept in large packs for hunting purposes. All dog packs have a leader and a social hierarchy in which each individual animal knows exactly its own place. Puppies are taught pack behavior by their mothers before they ever leave the whelping box. Pack behavior is just as significant for your Great Dane as for a wolf living in the wild. By understanding pack behavior, you can use it to help train your dog.

The "Alpha Male" Concept

Pack leadership always devolves on the strongest animal. In packs of dogs and wolves, the leader is generally an adult male in his prime with sufficient life experience to guide the pack in day-to-day survival. Because size and strength play a key part in this concept, and because male canines are usually larger and more powerful than the females, the leader of the pack is called the first or "alpha" male.

In the wild, the alpha male gets the best of the food and his choice of breeding-age females (usually known as the "alpha female"); his will is law in the pack. The alpha male zealously protects his pack and his leadership role from other canines, and he will oppose and possibly kill any serious challenger. The alpha male retains his position only as long as he is the smartest and strongest. When a stronger male comes along, the alpha male is deposed either by death or by exile from the pack.

Your Dane's best protection against accidents of all kinds is adequate training.

You, your family, and your Great Dane make up a pack. You or some other family member must assume alpha responsibilities and establish the hierarchy, with each male or female human ranking above the Great Dane. In the alpha role you have to be more dominant than the Dane. Establishing yourself in this role is much easier while your Dane is a puppy. It is possible to become the boss of an adult Great Dane, but if that dog itself has been in the top spot, a stubborn clash of wills results.

Because "nature hates a vacuum," if you or some other person in your family fail to take the alpha spot, your Dane may try to assume this position. Unless you can reassert your leadership and move the dog down several notches in the "pecking order," you have a difficult—if not potentially dangerous—situation. Imagine that you have a 150 pound (68 kg) canine tyrant in your home, one that will do only what it wants to do. You have the canine equivalent of the old joke about where an 800 pound gorilla sleeps—anywhere it wants to!

When to Begin Training

Some training has been begun for you by your Dane's mother. She instilled early lessons in her puppies while they were still unweaned babies. Her methods are good ones for you to follow in the further training of her son or daughter.

Repetition: Some behaviors were absolutely not tolerated and repeatedly brought instant correction.

Consistency: Bad behavior was corrected the same way each time. The mother didn't punish a particular act one time and reward it or ignore it the next time. Inconsistency only confuses a puppy.

Fairness: The correction was fair and not overly severe. The mother dog does not do a puppy any physical

harm for a youthful indiscretion. A snarl or a rough nudge from Mama is all most pups need to get the general idea that they did something wrong.

As long as the puppies were under her control, these lessons were enforced. If you follow this canine course in dog training, your job will be much easier, because it fits a pattern most Danes already understand. Training will have a more binding effect on the behavior of the dog. Repetition, consistency, and fairness worked for the mother, and that approach will work for you!

What Dog Training Is All About

Getting your Great Dane to do what you want it to do is not cruel, and it isn't a control game that you can use to show your friends and neighbors how you can manipulate a huge dog. Training your dog is as valuable for you and the members of your family as for the dog.

Before you can teach a dog, you have to decide what you want it to learn. You also have to decide on a "lesson plan" for handling what you want to teach and you have to understand what your dog can learn and how it learns before you can train it.

Although you may eventually teach your Great Dane a wide variety of cute, even amazing, tricks, your first priority is to teach the dog what it needs to know to be a better-functioning pet.

Housebreaking

Your Great Dane puppy started learning this important lesson when you first took the puppy to the designated spot to relieve itself, then enthusiastically praised it for doing so. Your pup was rewarded twice: once by the relief it got, and once by your praise.

Housebreaking a Great Dane puppy need not be arduous. Your puppy wants to please you. In this early part

Timing Trips Outside

Some understanding of puppy physiology is important. Knowing when your puppy normally needs to relieve itself allows you to establish a regular schedule for going outside. Here are some suggestions for timing trips outside:

• Take the puppy out to relieve itself after it eats.
• Go outside the first thing each morning, *immediately* after the puppy is released from the crate.
• Go out after the puppy naps during the day.
• Go out after a long and lively play period.
• Go out as late at night as possible.
• Go out immediately if the puppy shows signs of wanting to defecate or urinate: staying near the door, circling, sniffing, and looking generally uneasy.
• Always put on a leash if the Relief Place isn't inside a fenced backyard.

of your relationship you and your puppy are in complete agreement. Your part of the housebreaking task is to help your puppy please you by not making a mess inside. That is best achieved by understanding basic canine instinctual behavior and using this behavior to help your puppy learn its lesson.

No matter how much your Great Dane puppy may want to please you, until it is between three and four months of age it will have limited bladder control. Don't expect perfection until the pup matures enough physically to be able to delay relieving itself. But this is certainly not intended to suggest that you wait to begin housebreaking. The mental lesson needs to be firmly in place when the pup's physical functioning reaches maturity.

Crate training, the best and easiest way to help your dog become housebroken, takes advantage of a side effect of denning behavior. In the wild, animals rarely foul their dens. Not only would a soiled den be a messy, smelly place to live, but other predators could find it more easily by following the smell of accumulated urine and feces. It is for this reason that dogs, by nature, are reluctant to mess up their carrier/den (see Crate Training Suggestions, page 52).

Crate training takes advantage of the dog's innate desire to keep its den clean, but it requires a regular plan for puppy feeding and subsequent trips outside to the Relief Place. When crate training is used along with a feeding/relief trip plan and praise from you when the puppy does what you want, housebreaking becomes much simpler.

Sometimes you will get the puppy outside just in time. When the puppy relieves itself at the right place, elaborately praise it immediately. Stay with the puppy until it eliminates and receives its customary praise. This helps identify the act of relieving itself with the sights and smells of this particular place and with the reward it can expect for doing the right thing. *Never,* for any reason, scold the dog at this special spot! This is where it expects to do its business and then be rewarded. If you scare or punish the pup at this place, it may become confused by the conflicting messages you are sending.

If a puppy defecates or urinates inside, *never* strike it. A firm, alpha male-voiced *"No!"* will notify the puppy that this was not good behavior. *Never* make matters worse by rubbing the puppy's nose in urine or excrement. Such an illogical action does absolutely nothing to help the pup learn and may possibly cause it to fear you. You may be left with a messy puppy to clean up.

By feeding your Great Dane at regular times, you can usually anticipate the puppy's need to go outside. If you are using a highly digestible, premium puppy food, the pup's stools should be relatively firm and low in volume. If a mishap occurs, the mess isn't as bad to clean up. In addition, *never* feed a puppy table scraps, even in small amounts. They can upset a puppy's system and alter the balance of a quality food. Feed the puppy three or four times a day for approximately 15 minutes. Don't leave food out continuously.

While crate training is certainly the best form of housebreaking, it may not work well for people who can't stay home to help the pup adjust to a regular schedule of feeding and crate training. For owners who have to leave the puppy in a laundry room or a bathroom for the adjustment period, a second, perhaps not quite as effective, method of housebreaking is available: paper training. It does not work particularly well in combination with outside training because the puppy is given two "right" places to go, but paper training may be necessary for people who cannot stay constantly with the puppy in the first days. Paper training also works fairly well for people who live in multistory apartment buildings where getting a puppy outside quickly may not be easily achieved.

Paper training involves confining a puppy to some easily cleaned room, a bathroom, kitchen, or laundry room. Three basic areas are needed within the room designated for the pup's use: a den area where the puppy's carrier can be placed, a water and food area, and an elimination area. The elimination area should be covered with several layers of newspaper. The puppy will be encouraged to relieve itself on the paper. It should receive appropriate praise for going there. Since most dogs don't like to soil their food and water area any more than they want to mess up their den, the elimination area needs to be some distance away from the eating and sleeping places.

If there are several layers of newspaper, urine and excrement can be removed and disposed of by lifting the top layers. The puppy's scent will remain and remind the puppy of what it is to do here. You may have used old litter from the puppy's first home to "prime the pump" when teaching the puppy to eliminate outside at a special spot, and you can use the same trick to encourage use of the elimination section of the puppy's room. One way to move the growing pup from using the paper to eliminating outside is to gradually decrease the size of the elimination area and then gradually shift the process, paper and all, outside.

Paper training is usually a little slower method of housebreaking a puppy. Even with paper training, be sure to walk the puppy early each morning, late each night, and after meals when possible. Since your schedule prevents you from being with the puppy every time nature calls, the paper training method is only a stopgap way of helping your puppy until it has matured and gained more bladder and colon control.

If your puppy has an accident, get that area cleaned up as soon and as thoroughly as possible. Use an odor-removing cleaner to get rid of the pup's scent. If the smell lingers, the puppy may assume that this too is an acceptable site.

If you live in an urban area and your puppy must be walked on city streets and sidewalks, *always* pick up and dispose of any excrement. Not only is this responsible behavior, it is usually required by law!

HOW-TO:
Crate Training Suggestions

• Have a positive attitude toward cages, crates, and carriers. Take advantage of instinctual canine behavior in using such "dens" for your Great Dane.
• When you buy the crate or carrier, make sure it is large enough for the puppy to use as an adult. To keep the crate from being segmented by the puppy into a sleeping area and a relief area (much like the paper training room), install a sturdy partition to keep the den no larger than the puppy requires, and make the space bigger as the pup grows.
• Place the den in an out-of-the-way, but not isolated place in the home. Be sure that the crate is not in a direct draft or in the sun; otherwise, the puppy will not be comfortable.
• Put the Dane puppy in the crate for rest periods or when you have to leave the dog unattended for a few hours. Upon your return, immediately take the pup out to the relief spot, praise its activity there, and come right back in. If you want to go out and play, do so after the break is over, so that the dog will not confuse elimination with exercise or play.
• Do *not* enthusiastically praise or pet the pup for about 10 minutes after you let it out of the carrier to be with you indoors. Such praise may confuse the puppy and make it seem that getting out of the carrier is to be rewarded.
• Use a stern, tough alpha voice to quiet any crying or whining when the pup is returned to the carrier.
• Keep a mat or an old towel in the den along with a favorite toy or durable chew to keep the puppy occupied when awake.
• Never feed or water your Dane in its crate. The place for these activities is outside the denning area.
• Your family and friends need to understand the importance of the crate to your Dane pup's overall development. Don't let any member of the household upset the regimen that the puppy will become accustomed to after a few weeks.

The best method of keeping a Dane, or any other dog, inside is to have it crate-trained.

When to Start Training

A distinction is to be made between housebreaking, settling in, and other early lessons that your Great Dane puppy must learn and the more formal training that begins when the youngster is three to four months old. Although some dogs are ready a little earlier or a little later, at this age the Dane pup should be mature enough to actually gain something from basic obedience training. You are the key in that training. You must be consistent, confident, and patient if the commands you want to teach are to be learned. Training is not a family function until the five basic commands ("Sit," "Stay," "Heel," "Down," and "Come") have been thoroughly learned. One person must do the primary training, and it should be done the same way each time.

Training Equipment

As equipment for training your Dane, you will need a chain training collar (often miscalled a "choke chain"). This type of collar is both humane and effective when correctly and appropriately used. The chain collar, which is to be worn only during training sessions, does not choke the dog. When correcting pressure is applied, the collar causes the dog's head to come up with a slight snap. This gets the dog's attention. When applied in conjunction with the stern "No," it not only controls and corrects, but also lets the pup know that its action was undesirable.

The chain collar should be large enough to go over your Dane puppy's head at its widest part with no more than an inch of extra room. This collar *must* be removed after training and replaced with a regular collar, which may have identification and rabies vaccination tags attached. The puppy or dog should associate the training collar with training. If an unat-

tended dog should snag such a collar on something, strangulation could occur when the frightened animal tries to escape.

Along with the training collar you will need a 1 inch (2.5 cm) wide leash (sometimes called a lead) measuring 6 feet (1.8 m) in length. This leash, not to be used on your regular walks with the dog, should be made of leather, nylon, or woven web with a sturdy but comfortable hand loop on one end. The leash should have a securely attached swivel snap for attaching to the ring on the chain training collar.

Let your Dane puppy become thoroughly familiar with the chain training collar and the training leash. The dog must not fear these training aids if they are to work effectively. Let the puppy gradually get used to the weight and feel of both on its neck for several days before you actually begin training.

The Five Key Commands

Before you begin to teach your pup, you need to learn to give commands effectively:

Be firm: Issue clear, one-word commands to your dog, and use the dog's name before each command to get its attention: "Don, sit." Be authoritative: do not use baby talk or endearments. You can play with the pup later, but now you should be about the business of training!

Be consistent: Use the same tone of voice each time, so that your pup will know by the intonation as well as by the words that you mean business.

Be specific: Don't confuse the dog by issuing several commands at one time: "Don, come here and sit down." Each command has a single, specific word, and that word should be used each time and in the same tone of voice.

Training tip: Remember the canine learning rules and use them:

1. Praise enthusiastically;
2. Correct fairly and immediately;
3. Practice consistent repetition;
4. Never, never lose your temper;
5. Be patient.

The last rule deserves additional discussion. Don't take your pup out for a training session when you are angry about something. The puppy can hear the underlying hostility in your voice and may think that it is to be punished. Training should be based on correction and praise, not on punishment. Wait until you are less emotionally charged before you work with the Dane puppy.

Keep lessons short, no more than 20 minutes. Teach one new command at a time. Your pup will be doing well to learn all these commands over a period of months; don't try to build Rome in a day. When the training session is over, don't immediately begin playing and roughhousing with your Great Dane; let 20 minutes go by to separate training time with the authoritarian from playtime with the friend.

Other members of the household need to understand that the training of the puppy is serious business. They also need to understand the basics of what you are doing with the pup, so that they will not inadvertently undo your training when they play with the dog.

Sit

The "sit" command is a good starting point for your Great Dane because it already knows how to sit down. All you need to do is to teach it when and where to do so. With the training collar attached to the training leash, place the puppy on your left side next to your left leg, while holding the leash in your right hand. In one continuous motion, gently pull the pup's head up as you push its hindquarters down with your left hand, giving the firm command "Sit" as you do so.

When the pup is in the sitting position, lavishly praise it. Using the concept of continuous repetition, practice this lesson until the puppy sits down without having its rear end pushed downward. Remember to keep the same upward tension on the lead to keep the "sit" from becoming a belly flop. If the puppy shifts to the left or right, use your left hand to move it back in line gently, but firmly. Practice this lesson until your Great Dane associates the word "sit" and your firm tone with the lavish praise it will receive if it sits down. Soon the puppy will sit upon hearing the command, without either the downward push of its rear end or the upward pull of its head. After each successful "sit," praise the puppy liberally to ensure that the praise and its cause stand out in your puppy's memory.

Keep training sessions brief. Don't leave the youngster in the sitting position long enough for it to get bored. Gradually

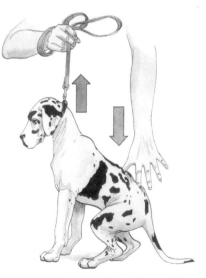

In one continuous, gentle motion, pull the pup's head up as you push its hindquarters down with your left hand, giving the firm verbal command "Sit" as you do so.

increase the time for sitting, always using consistent repetition and the praise reward to help your puppy learn. Several brief, consistent sessions will be much more effective than one long one.

Stay

Do not attempt to teach the "stay" command until your Dane puppy has thoroughly learned the "sit." The stay is begun from the sit; without that foundation, the stay cannot be mastered.

To begin the stay command, place your dog in the regular sitting position on your left. Keep some tension on the lead in your right hand to keep your pup's head up. Giving the clear, authoritative command "Stay," step away from the dog (moving your right foot first). At the same time, bring the palm of your left hand down in front of your Dane's face. Your command, the stepping away (always starting on the right foot), and the hand signal *must* occur at exactly the same time and in exactly the same way each time.

Maintain eye contact with your dog and repeat the "stay" command in the same firm tone as before. Do this several times, but don't expect long stays at first. Praise the puppy for its stays, but if it moves toward you, calmly take it back to the starting point, make it sit, and begin again with consistent repetition of the "stay" command. If the puppy seems to have trouble with stays, don't tire it by repeating this command over and over. Your puppy naturally wants to be near you, an impulse that this command thwarts. At the end of each short session, if your puppy hasn't caught on to the stay yet, finish up with a few sits, with a good reward for each one, thus ending the training time on a positive note. Be patient with your Great Dane and it *will* learn the stay.

Once the puppy can handle the stay command, praise it enthusiastically. Soon you will be able to move gradually farther and farther away, and the puppy

Giving the clear, firm command "Stay," you step away from the dog, moving your right foot first. At the same time you bring the palm of your left hand down in front of the pup's face.

will not move. Introduce the release word "okay" in a cheerful, happy tone when you want the puppy to stop staying and to return to you for its reward.

Heel

Once the puppy has mastered the sit and the stay and feels comfortable with the training collar and leash, you can begin to teach the "heel." Begin the heel command with your Great Dane in the sit position on your left, with the pup's head in line with your left foot. Holding the training leash in your right hand and leading off with your left foot, step forward while saying in a firm voice, "Heel." As with the other commands, use the pup's name to begin: "Don, heel."

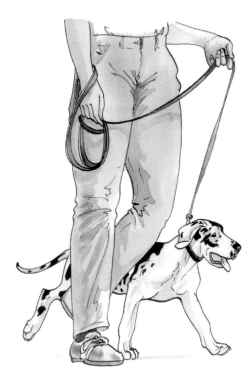

Holding the training leash in your right hand and leading off with your left foot, step forward while calling the dog by name and saying firmly "Heel."

with your dog, but to position the dog on your left and teach it to move when you move and stop when you stop. The ultimate goal of teaching the heel command is to get your Great Dane to heel without use of the leash.

Never drag your puppy around just to cover ground. If your pup has trouble with the heel, go back to the sit and start again. The heel may be hard for some dogs to learn, but continue your use of consistent tugs on the leash to keep your Dane moving, and keep its head in line with your left leg. Through consistent repetition, correction, and reward, your dog will learn to heel.

Down

"Down" begins with the "sit" and the "stay." Do not use the upward pull of the sit and stay, but pull down on the lead with your right hand, presenting the palm of your left hand in a downward motion while giving the strong command "Down." If the dog is reluctant to lie down as you want it to do, run the lead under your left foot and pull up on it gently, which will force the dog's head down. Remember to repeat both the hand signal and the voice command in exactly the same way each time.

Once the puppy is in the down position, pour on the praise. You can help your pup in the beginning by using your left hand much as when you teach the sit, only instead of pushing down on the hindquarters, you push down on the back while pulling on the lead to make the dog go down on its stomach. It is the downward direction that this command emphasizes, but it should also be used with the "stay." The ultimate goal is to cause the puppy to go straight down on its stomach at your command and to remain there until released by an "okay" from you.

The down can be a very useful and potentially important command for your young Dane. It can stop the dog in its tracks when it might be headed

If the puppy doesn't move out with you, pop the leash loudly against the side of your leg and repeat the command, walking away as you do so. When the puppy gets the idea and catches up with you, praise it but keep moving forward. Continue the praise and encouragement as long as your Dane stays with you in the proper alignment.

When you stop, give the command to sit. Once your Great Dane becomes comfortable with heeling, it will sit on its own when you stop. Don't let the dog run ahead, lag behind, or swivel around to face you. The purpose of the heel command is not only to walk

toward some danger. Continue to practice the down with the sit and stay, and thoroughly reward the dog with lavish praise when it stays put in the down position. By the use of patience and consistent repetition, you should be able to gradually increase the length of the down and even to leave your dog's line of sight and expect it to remain in place.

Come

The "come" command may seem both obvious and easy, but there are several important elements to it. Your enthusiasm and use of the dog's name while giving the command "Come" with your arms held out wide will assure your puppy that you really want it to come to you.

Always lavish praise on the puppy, even though it is doing something it wants to do. Use the training leash to give the dog little tugs if it doesn't come directly to you in a straight line. The "come" is another command that you want obeyed immediately, not after the dog has had a chance to mark a post or watch a butterfly. Treat the come like other commands; be peremptory, and use the pup's name. Danes can sometimes be stubborn or inattentive, but the command in combination with the gentle but firm tugs on the lead should help your Dane pup master this task. After the pup has mastered coming to you from the end of the 6 foot (1.8 m) leash you can switch to a longer one—up to 20 feet (6 m)—to reinforce the idea that the command means to come from any distance, not just a few feet away. Always reward the dog with liberal petting and praise when it comes to you.

The "come" command is different from the other basic obedience commands. It does not have to be repeated over and over again in a session. Also, you can use the come unexpectedly in play sessions or when the dog is walking in the backyard. However, you should always expect an immediate response from the dog, and it should always expect a reward of praise from you.

Never make the mistake of many dog owners who call a dog to come and then scold or punish it for some action! That teaches the dog that "Sometimes when I go to the Boss I get punished," and it raises doubt in the dog's mind about whether a reward or a reprimand will be the outcome of obeying. If a dog needs to be corrected for something, *go to the dog* and correct it; don't confuse the dog's natural impulse to come to you!

The Importance of Obedience Classes for You and Your Dane

If you have never trained a dog before, you may discover that a dog training class helps you and your young Great Dane become more accomplished. Not only are these classes taught by experts who can help you help your dog learn, but they also give you a chance to spend some away-from-home time with your dog in the company of other dogs and their owners. If your pup shows any inclination to aggressiveness or stubbornness, a training class (held several times a year in communities all over the country) may be just what you need to move your dog in the right behavioral direction. Ask the breeder of your puppy for recommendations of classes or teachers. You could find that such a class would be not only helpful, but also fun!

These young Danes cannot reach their potential as good companion dogs without proper training. Don't own an untrained Dane!

When this fawn Dane puppy grows into its feet, it will be a giant dog.

Feeding Your Great Dane

The Importance of a Good Diet

All dogs need and deserve food that meets their nutritional needs, that they enjoy eating, and that can be offered in consistent and convenient ways. Diet is especially important for giant dogs like the Great Dane. Although some breeds and types of dogs can get by on average foods, Great Danes and other rapidly growing breeds must have a good diet if they are to achieve their genetic potential.

Without a good diet Great Danes cannot attain their huge size and impressive musculature. Dogs that are neglected nutritionally may also suffer in their mental development. Since your dog will have to depend on you for what it eats, it is important that you understand what is needed by your Dane and why.

Special Feeding Considerations

Although opinions vary among Great Dane breeders, there seems to be some validity to the idea that feeding young Great Danes (or other fast-growing breeds) is much more difficult than feeding their average-sized cousins. Rapidly growing dogs, if fed a diet too high in protein, may put on muscle and tissue faster than their skeletal structures can grow to support the weight. Excesses and imbalances of calcium and phosphorus can lead to bone growth abnormalities in Danes and other giant breeds.

The other extreme—a diet too low in protein—is just as bad. Without suffi-cient protein for the muscles and tis-sues to develop, the Dane can remain spindly and lack the typical physique of the "Apollo of Dogdom." Without proper guidance and understanding, the attempt to feed your Dane appro-priately can become a two-edged sword—either you give it so much that the bones suffer, or you don't give it enough to put on sufficient flesh.

Not only does a giant dog need an elevat-ed feeding dish, but it also needs a height-ened awareness on the part of its owner about what is and what isn't good nutrition for a rapidly growing Great Dane.

The Elements of Good Canine Nutrition

There are eight components or elements that make up a sound nutritional feeding program for your Great Dane. If any one of these elements is neglected or ignored, your dog's diet cannot be described as either sound or balanced. These elements are: protein (keeping in mind the special needs or constraints of a rapidly growing youngster); carbohydrates; fats; vitamins; minerals; water; owner knowledge; and owner consistency.

The best solution to this quandary may come from your Dane mentor or from the breeder of the puppy you have purchased. Since certain strains or families within a breed may metabolize food differently from others, try to follow the lead of the experts who know the lineage of your dog. If the breeder of your puppy has had success in raising related puppies to adulthood using a specific dog food with a set protein level, by all means try to stay with that food or one very like it.

Balance—The Key to Good Nutrition

Because our dogs are totally dependent on us for all the food they ingest, we must be absolutely certain that the diets we use are balanced. Balanced dog foods are scientifically formulated to contain all the necessary protein, carbohydrates, fats, vitamins, and minerals your Great Dane needs to grow to giant proportions and then maintain an active, healthy metabolism.

The food must contain the right blend of the right things. Far too many dog owners are content to feed whatever is handy, available, expedient, and inexpensive. As a Dane owner, you need different criteria. You must find high-quality food that meets the requirements of your Great Dane. The food has to be not only balanced, but also palatable—your dog must willing to eat it!

There are a few major rules to follow in determining a successful feeding plan for your Dane. To avoid a poor diet and to establish a nutritionally sound feeding regimen, adhere to these basic principles:

Quality: Feed your Great Dane a premium quality, nutritionally balanced dog food, and understand why it is such.

Consistency: As long as a particular food is meeting your dog's needs, stick with it. Don't jump around from brand to brand.

Suitability: Don't overfeed, and *avoid table scraps!* There is no way to keep your Dane's diet balanced if the household leftovers end up in the dog's stomach. Dog food is balanced for dogs, not for humans, and the reverse is also true—human food will not meet the dog's nutritional needs.

Protein

Protein provides your Great Dane with the key amino acids that are so necessary for your dog's progression through the formative stages of its life; the continued sustaining of healthy bone and muscle; the body's own repair functions on bone and muscle; the production of infection-fighting antibodies; and the production of needed hormones and enzymes that aid in natural chemical processes within the dog's body.

There are a variety of good sources of protein in dog food. In the guaranteed analysis percentages required on pet food packaging, protein is listed first. Because protein needs are crucial and sometimes difficult to gauge with growing Great Danes, follow the example of those who have had success raising youngsters closely related to yours and you too should be successful.

Carbohydrates

Carbohydrates supply fuel for your Great Dane's physical motor. Thoroughly cooked grain and vegetable products, in company with processed starches, provide most of the carbohydrates in premium-quality pet foods. Along with fats, carbohydrates are the elements in your Dane's diet that furnish usable energy. Carbohydrates are measured in calories.

Fats

The fats in your pet's diet are a more concentrated energy source than carbohydrates. In fact, an amount of fat will provide *twice* as much usable energy as an equal amount of carbohydrates. The key vitamins A, D, E, and K are delivered by the fats in your Great Dane's meals, and these "fat soluble" vitamins help develop and maintain healthy skin and coat.

Fats are of special importance in maintaining a dog's nervous system and equally significant in making dog foods palatable. Dog foods that taste good are more readily eaten by dogs. Further, fat levels are often measured against the general activity level of a dog, with the stresses of obedience work, breeding, and the show ring requiring more fats than the routine of a less active dog.

Vitamins

While vitamins are certainly needed by your Great Dane for the general functioning of its body, they are one of those good things that easily can be overdone. All the vitamins a dog normally needs are supplied in a regular diet of premium-quality dog food. Unless your veterinarian indicates otherwise, *don't* add to the vitamin levels of a good food. Not only do additional vitamins generally do no good, but they can actually do harm.

Minerals

Minerals are important to the normal functioning of your dog. Calcium and phosphorus are needed to develop and sustain healthy bones, teeth, and muscles. Sodium and potassium help maintain normal levels of canine body fluids and a healthy nervous system. Like vitamins, minerals are not needed in huge amounts in your dog's regular diet; they usually are adequately provided by consistent feeding of a good-quality dog food.

Water

Clean, fresh water is vitally important to the health of your Great Dane. Your dog needs lots of good water available at all times. Poor-quality, bacteria- or algae-filled water is not going to be drunk in the needed amounts by your pet. Make water as crucial a part of your pet's diet as any other. Keep water bowls full, disinfected, and readily available.

Owner Knowledge

Feeding a giant dog entails giant responsibilities. Not only do rapidly growing young Danes need different rations from average-sized breeds, but your Great Dane's health throughout its life may also largely depend on your knowledge of the food you feed it. Your Dane is totally dependent on you for everything it regularly eats. Your awareness of its nutritional requirements and the foods that best meet those needs is a major part—perhaps the key part—of your obligation to your pet.

Owner Consistency

Unfortunately, the diet of many dogs in this country is determined by whatever is on sale at the nearest convenience store. Most dogs can survive on such constant variety, but they will not thrive on such a practice. This is especially true of the Great Dane.

Find a food that meets the needs of your dog reasonably well, and stick with it. If your dog knows what food it can expect, it is less likely to be a picky eater and its system will adjust to the formula of this particular diet. It is a human idea, not a canine one, that dogs love variety. Your pet will do better on the same high-quality food, fed at regular times, throughout much of its life.

Commercial Dog Foods

Find a good dog food. Stick with it. Don't overfeed. Avoid table scraps like the plague.

There are hundreds of pet food products available. Some are high-quality, balanced foods that may be just what you and your Great Dane are seeking. Others are inferior products that are best avoided by a dog owner in search of a nutritionally complete diet for a special pet.

Part of the owner-knowledge component of your Great Dane's feeding plan is your learning how to read a dog food label and how to use this information in your pet's best interest. Along with the guaranteed analysis (which lists percentages of protein, fats, fiber, and moisture), there is a list of the ingredients of the dog food. The first ingredient listed is the one most prevalent in the food, the second is the next highest in amount, and so forth.

Also on the label should be the manufacturer's recommended feeding amounts, based on the weight of the dog fed. Generally based on averages, they do not take into account the special feeding needs of giant dogs. Talk with your veterinarian and with experienced Dane breeders about the amounts right for your dog.

One of the pluses of using a premium-quality food is that its manufacturer normally has a toll-free number that can connect you with people experienced in canine nutrition. Don't hesitate to use the number to ascertain what food to feed or to ask questions about a food your Dane is already being fed.

Commercial dog foods generally come in three main forms: canned, semimoist, and dry. Each type has distinct advantages and disadvantages.

Canned Dog Food

Canned dog food (sometimes called wet food) is the most palatable and the most expensive way to feed your Great Dane. Canned food generally smells really good to a dog and usually is eaten with gusto, but because of its high moisture rating of 75 to 85 percent it can also spoil quickly, even at room temperature. For a giant dog, a diet of canned food exclusively could be quite an expensive proposition. Additionally, the resultant stool firmness and odor are usually the most unsatisfactory of the three forms of dog food.

Canned food is convenient and its long shelf life makes it easy to keep, but a steady diet of canned food tends to create more dental problems than dry dog food. Most canned food is used as an additive, or mixer, with dry dog food for really large breeds of dogs.

Semimoist Dog Food

Many of the semimoist dog foods come in shapes that appeal to human buyers rather than dogs. Patties, chops, and other meaty-looking configurations are used to sell the product, not to make it more nutritious or acceptable to a pet. Semimoist dog food is generally quite palatable and has a reasonably good storage life. It is expensive for big dogs to eat exclusively, but it can be mixed with dry foods.

The stool quality with semimoist foods is a little better than with canned foods, but less satisfactory than with dry foods. Semimoist foods, which usually have a moisture rating of about 30 percent, are not used as a main diet by many Great Dane breeders. One advantage of semimoist food is the product's suitability as a treat or as a meal for a dog whose regular appetite is a bit off.

Dry Dog Food

Dry dog food is the most cost-effective and most popular form of dog food, especially among large dog breeders. There are a good many dry foods on the market that can be described as complete dog diets with proper nutritional balance.

Dry foods (unlike partially used canned and semimoist foods) also keep well without refrigeration. Dry foods are somewhat less palatable, and dogs that have been fed only canned, semimoist, or table-scrap diets may have to be taught to eat dry foods.

Because dry dog foods require more use of a pet's teeth, they contribute to better dental health and tartar reduction. (Note: Information from some dry dog food makers notwithstanding, dry food alone is not enough to keep your dog's teeth in good shape. See page 79).

The stool quality obtained with premium-quality dry food is usually the most satisfactory. Digestibility is usually quite good, and puppies started on dry food continue to eat it readily all their lives. Dry dog food, however, has a moisture rating of only about 10 percent, so the need for good, fresh water for your Great Dane is all the greater.

Homemade Diets and Leftovers

Many dog breeders with years of experience develop their own concoctions for their pets. Unless you are a trained canine nutritionist or a dog breeder with great experience and relevant knowledge, leave homemade diets alone. In the best of hands they may work as well as many commercial foods. Prepared by novices or ill-informed owners, however, homemade diets are little more than nutritionally lacking meals of disguised table scraps.

Do your pet a favor: Until you can do as good a job of canine diet formulation as the companies that have spent millions of dollars and decades of research developing their products, let the experts make the dog food!

Treats

As a rule, table scraps have absolutely no place in a balanced canine diet. Such ill-considered snacks can keep a dog from eating the right amount of its balanced food or even throw the regular diet's balance completely out of kilter. Feeding table scraps to your Great Dane also may cause the big dog to expect to eat not only what you do, but when you do, and possibly where you do. Your dog should eat from its dish at the regular time that you ordain.

Dog biscuits: Among the treats that can be given safely and appropriately to your Great Dane are quality dog biscuits. Such biscuits not only are nutritionally good for Dane's diet, but also are balanced to fit into the dog's regular diet. Follow the same rules with biscuits that you do with dog food; find a kind the dog likes and stay with it. Don't overfeed the biscuits; a few are enough.

Chews: Non-food items like the various nylon, rubber, and rawhide articles do not necessarily fall into the category of treats. They are, however, good for your dog. Besides providing some benefit in tartar removal (not to replace regular dental care), these items also give a teething puppy or a bored adult a suitable alternative to the furniture.

Feeding Great Dane Puppies (Under Two Years Old)

Other than the concerns about rapidly growing young Danes, which

This brindle Great Dane will need a balanced diet to grow big and strong and stay healthy.

you can probably resolve by following the advice of veteran Dane owners and your veterinarian, feeding Dane puppies isn't that different from feeding puppies of other breeds.

Tip: When you bring your Dane pup home, by all means get some of the same food it was fed at the breeder's. By continuing the puppy on the same food, you reduce the transition stress that begins when your puppy leaves the only home it has ever known and moves to yours!

Young puppies need to be fed about four times a day with a quality food. As they grow older, the number of feedings can drop to three and finally to two as they approach adulthood. There may be other formats for feeding certain strains or families of Danes. Your Dane mentor can help you find a schedule that meets both your pup's needs and yours.

Feeding Adult Great Danes (Over Two Years Old)

For some dogs adulthood comes more quickly than for others. There are those who believe that a Great Dane is near maturity at a little over one year. Because skeletal growth may be surpassed by muscular growth, feeding still-maturing youngsters according to the strict suggestions of experienced Dane owners and canine nutrition experts seems wise.

Normally an adult dog receives two feedings a day. The amount and the number of daily feedings also depend on the special circumstances that affect you and your Dane. If your Dane is a prime show dog being actively campaigned at different locations each weekend, its needs differ from those of a spayed or neutered Dane that lives a more sedentary existence as a pet. The metabolism of some dogs, even littermates, may be such that they need more food than others. You can gauge this only by living with and observing the food needs of your pet.

Feeding Older Danes (Five Years Old and Older)

As your Dane reaches its "golden" years, its metabolism may begin to slow down. At this point in life, the dog needs more carbohydrates and less fat in its food. There are any number of dog foods designed for older canines. These should be useful for your Great Dane, if fed moderately and consistently.

Spayed and neutered Danes usually require a diet much like that of older dogs, regardless of the pet's age. The point to remember in feeding older pets, spays, and neuters is that a fat Dane is not a healthy Dane. Not only does added weight make the dog's internal organs work harder, but a large, obese dog also puts more pressure on its feet, legs, and joints. Ask your veterinarian and other Dane owners how to feed dogs in this group.

When You Change Dog Foods

Although experts disagree on the length of time you should take to introduce a dog food change, one good way is to effect this dietetic transition over a month's time. This method stresses gradual change. The first week of the month, feed 75 percent of the current food with 25 percent of the new brand. Observe the dog's acceptance of the new ration. If the new food seems to cause no problems, feed 50 percent of each kind for the second and third weeks. The fourth week, mix 25 percent of the old with 75 percent of the new. You should be able to start the next month on the entirely new diet. Change your Dane's food slowly, and you'll achieve better results.

Your Great Dane and Medical Care

Giant Dogs Have Different Health Needs

Like other aspects of Great Dane ownership, medical care of a giant dog brings special concerns. Not every owner can even get an immobile or unconscious dog weighing well over 100 pounds (45 kg) *into* an automobile to take it to a veterinary clinic. Not every veterinarian feels equally comfortable with every breed of dog.

Keeping Your Great Dane Healthy

Your Great Dane deserves and needs a team of concerned, knowledgeable people to make and keep its existence a safe one. This team will include you, the other members of your family, a trusted, experienced Dane breeder (serving as your Dane's friend and your mentor), and—of greatest value—your Great Dane's veterinarian.

You and your family should study accident prevention techniques and concepts and learn about parasites, disease, and other medical conditions that may afflict your pet.

An experienced Dane owner can offer valuable help and advice at almost every step. An experienced friend is in an excellent position to judge the overall external physical condition of your pet. By being close enough to the dog to know it well, yet outside the everyday household, your mentor can provide an aware yet slightly detached viewpoint. Certain gradual changes in appearance and condition will be more visible to this friendly outsider than to a member of the household.

While the family is the major molding force in your Great Dane's health and well being, and the mentor is a good source of information and perspective, it is your veterinarian who plays the key role in your dog's health plan. No one is better able to keep your Dane in good shape or to get it back into good shape in the event of a medical problem.

Choosing a veterinarian for your Great Dane is an important decision. Most veterinary practitioners are skillful, caring professionals who offer sound care and treatment to their animal patient and solid information and guidance to their patient's owners. For your Great Dane, you need a little more. The health needs of giant dogs are somewhat different from those of most other dogs. Try to find a veterinarian who not only has experience with a number of the "giant" breeds (Danes, Irish wolfhounds, Saint Bernards, mastiffs, Great Pyrenees, Newfoundlands) but likes big dogs as well.

Preventive Care

Prevention of medical problems is always better than an after-the-fact treatment approach. Because Great Danes are huge dogs, they can have huge problems. Preventing health problems in such a giant breed involves several diverse aspects of Dane ownership.

The harlequin is among the most difficult colors to breed correctly in all of the dog world.

HOW-TO:
Preventing Health Problems

Sound breeding: Choosing a Dane from physically and temperamentally sound stock is an essential element in an effort to avoid painful, expensive, and heart-rending circumstances later. No dog can be absolutely guaranteed to be free of serious medical problems during its life. Choosing a puppy or an adult Great Dane with a potentially heritable medical problem in its pedigree increases the likelihood of problems.

Training: Failing to prepare adequately for a rapidly maturing canine of a giant breed increases the probability of accidents, and from these accidents dire consequences can result. For example, the assumption that your Dane will always be a model canine and never get into trouble when running free in a neighborhood is ludicrous. If you don't have your dog under some form of control or restraint at *all* outside times (a fence or a leash, in combination *with* good training), medical problems—perhaps fatal ones—are *certain* to come your dog's way.

Regular medical care: Regular physical examinations by a licensed veterinary practitioner will not only identify many existing medical conditions, but also spot potential problems that can be avoided with preventive care. No dog should go without immunizations and regular check-ups.

Nutrition: Because of the demand placed on the metabolism, bones, and muscle tissue

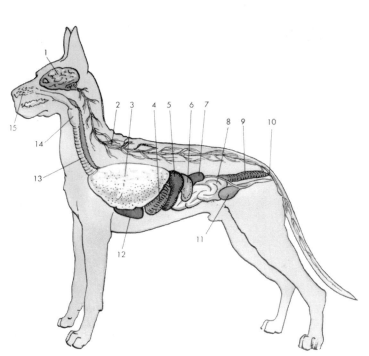

The major internal organs of the Great Dane: *1. brain 2. spinal cord 3. lungs 4. liver 5. stomach 6. spleen 7. kidney 8. small intestine 9. colon 10. anus 11. bladder 12. heart 13. trachea 14. larynx 15. sinus cavity*

of a rapidly growing Great Dane, owners must become well versed in dog nutrition generally and in Dane nutrition specifically. Failure to do so can result in an adult Great Dane that does not reach its full genetic potential or, in the worst case, has skeletal deformities and painful disabilities requiring euthanasia.

Preparation: Hoping for the best while preparing for the worst is a sound philosophy for a novice Dane owner. Even with the best of care, feeding, medical attention, training, and a safety-oriented environment, a puppy or an adult dog can become injured or sick. While a good working relationship with a

Dane-aware veterinarian is part of an emergency plan, there are other factors to be considered.

• Unless you are as large a human as your Dane is a dog, you may need help getting your sick or injured pet to the veterinary office. Not everyone will be willing or able to provide this help on the spur of the moment. Plan for such circumstances, hoping that they will never occur.

• Knowledge of possible Dane-threatening conditions, like gastric tortion (or bloat), is a mandatory precondition for becoming the owner of a Great Dane. Learn about these conditions and what to do if such problems should occur.

66

Immunizations and the Diseases They Control

Not only are inoculations against an array of dog-harming or dog-killing diseases a pivotal part of your Great Dane's preventive health plan, but in most places some of these illness-fighting shots are also required by law!

Your Great Dane puppy may have had its first immunizations at about six weeks of age while still at the breeder's. These initial shots were vaccinations for distemper and measles and possibly for parvovirus, canine hepatitis, leptospirosis, parainfluenza, coronavirus, and bordetella.

Don't believe for a second that this initial round of inoculations completes your pup's immunization requirements. To prevent these diseases properly, follow-up shots are given usually at 8 to 10 weeks, again at 12 weeks, and finally at 16 to 18 weeks. Rabies inoculations are given between three and six months of age. Annual boosters are needed for some shots.

The shot record should be a part of the permanent paperwork you obtain when you get a puppy or an adult

The skeleton of a Great Dane shows the strong framework on which this giant dog must rest. Emphasis among Dane breeders centers on not letting the body outgrow the skeleton and cause crippling conditions.

Great Dane. Your pet's veterinarian needs to know what vaccinations (or other treatments) your dog received before you became its owner. This complete accounting of what has been done to and for your Great Dane will form the foundation of your pet's health records, which should be kept current and accurate throughout the life of the dog.

Your veterinarian will set up a schedule for these life-saving shots. Your diligence in seeing that your young Dane is on hand to get its immunizations is the key to the good health of your puppy. If you forget or neglect this important task, you put your pet at great risk.

Distemper

Distemper has a long history of tragic consequences. Once the deadliest threat to puppies and young dogs, this extremely infectious and widely spread viral disease affects dogs and all other canines, as well as some other warm-blooded animals. Raging through kennels some decades ago, distemper could kill a majority of the young dogs and all of the puppies. Once infected with distemper, some kennels could never recover and were forced out of business.

Veterinary medicine subsequently developed an immunization program that has greatly lowered the rate of occurrence of this dread killer, but the inoculations work only if administered properly and renewed annually! Distemper still occurs in places where dogs are not adequately vaccinated or in feral canine and other wild animal populations.

A dog not adequately immunized can show clinical signs as soon as a week after coming into contact with an animal infected with distemper. Initially distemper appears as a cold with a runny nose and a little fever. In most cases, the dog "goes off its feed" or stops eating altogether. Listlessness, fatigue, and diarrhea are observed in most dogs.

Veterinary medicine has done much to eliminate distemper from the lives of dogs and dog owners. Vaccination and yearly booster shots have made this killer of puppies and young dogs much less of a threat.

The muscles and sinews of the Great Dane show a canine athlete of great power and substance.

Rabies

Very few other diseases can evoke the same level of fear as rabies, the dreaded "madness" of hydrophobia. Mental pictures of once faithful dogs turning into mouth-foaming, raging monsters are still entrenched in the minds of people who remember when most pets were not inoculated against this infectious, fatal disease.

Rabies is most often transmitted by the saliva of an infected animal through bite wounds. Most warm-blooded mammals, including human beings, can be victims of rabies, but it is most often spread by skunks, bats, raccoons, foxes, horses, cows, unvaccinated cats and dogs, and other small animals.

In some places, rabies is relatively widespread. Other countries, like England, have effectively eradicated rabies through a widespread prevention program and strict quarantine restrictions. Until 1885, when Louis Pasteur developed the first vaccine against rabies, the disease meant certain death. Rabies presents certain classic signs, the first of which is the symptom that gave the disease the descriptive name hydrophobia, "a fear of water." Rabies virus infection causes paralysis of the laryngeal muscles that control swallowing. In later stages of the disease, the victim is unable to swallow; excessive salivation causes the "foaming at the mouth" that is a well-known warning sign. The infected mammal is unable and "afraid" to drink water (or anything else). Two phases are usually seen. In the first, furious phase the animal will attack anything and everything around it. Sometimes the infected animal dies in this phase, but if not, rabies progresses into the second phase—the dumb or more inactive stage—which ends in paralysis, coma, and death.

A Great Dane is a large and generally active dog. Rabies in such a pet would represent a significant threat to you, your family, and others. Immunization at three to six months, with another inoculation at the age of one year followed by annual rabies shots thereafter, will protect your Dane from this horrible and unnecessary death.

Leptospirosis

This bacterial disease, which primarily damages the kidneys, is commonly spread by drinking or coming into contact with water contaminated by the urine of an infected animal. Clinical signs of leptospirosis are loss of appetite, fever, vomiting and diarrhea, and abdominal pain.

In advanced cases, leptospirosis can severely damage the liver and kidneys, with resultant jaundice, weakened hindquarters, mouth sores, and weight loss. Immunization for leptospirosis and annual booster shots are usually enough to protect your Great Dane.

Hepatitis

Infectious canine hepatitis, which can affect any member of the canine family, can be contracted by dogs at any age. The severity of hepatitis (which is not the illness of the same name that affects humans) ranges from a relatively mild sickness to a quickly fatal viral infection that can take the life of an infected dog within 24 hours of the onset of the illness.

The symptoms of infectious canine hepatitis can include listlessness, fever, blood in stools and vomitus, abdominal pain, light sensitivity of the eyes, and tonsillitis. As an infectious disease, hepatitis can be spread by contact with the feces or urine of an infected animal. Immunization with a yearly booster is a good preventive measure.

Parvovirus

This viral disease is a serious killer, especially of puppies, but it can mean death to an unvaccinated or untreated dog at any age. Parvovirus primarily attacks the bone marrow, immune system, and gastrointestinal tract, but it can also damage the heart. Puppies with parvovirus can suffer from severe dehydration because of profuse bloody, watery diarrhea and vomiting and may die within 48 hours of the onset of the disease.

While good veterinary care can save some parvovirus victims, immunization is a much better course of action. If your unimmunized Great Dane puppy were to encounter a parvovirus-infected dog, a debilitating disease with potentially fatal consequences could result. Puppy vaccination followed by annual follow-up shots should keep parvovirus away from your pet.

Parainfluenza

Parainfluenza is a highly infectious viral disease that can rage through a dog population, as in a kennel or home where several dogs live. It is thought to be spread by contact with infected animals and the places they live, as well through the air. Parainfluenza causes a condition called tracheobronchitis, which is usually identified by a dry, hacking cough followed by retching as an attempt to cough up throat mucus. In and of itself, parainfluenza is not usually a serious illness. Untreated, however, tracheobronchitis can weaken a dog and make it vulnerable to other ailments and infections.

Parainfluenza is preventable by vaccination in the puppy series with annual reinoculation. Treatment for this disease is best administered by a veterinarian, with the patient isolated from other dogs to decrease the chances of further contagion.

A mother needs extra nutrition for herself and her growing puppies.

Coronavirus

Dogs of any age can be affected by this contagious disease, which can cause severe diarrhea with watery, loose, foul-smelling, bloody stools. The disease caused by coronavirus is similar to that caused by parvovirus, and it may leave a dog in such a weakened condition that parvovirus or other infections may occur.

Treatment by your Great Dane's veterinarian can be successful, but immunization by vaccine is the preferred course. By preventing this ailment, you may be able to avoid putting your pet at risk for more serious medical problems.

Bordetella

Bordetella is a bacterial infection often found in association with tracheobronchitis. Bordetella may make treatment of the parainfluenza-induced tracheobronchitis more difficult. Protect your Dane from this infectious "fellow-traveler" by providing your pet with the immunization that does much to prevent its occurrence.

Borelliosis (Lyme Disease)

Borelliosis, or Lyme disease, is a serious, potentially fatal disease that affects warm-blooded animals and humans. Since your Great Dane may walk in parks or other wooded areas, the possibility of exposure to Lyme disease must be considered. The ailment can even be contracted in your pet's own backyard.

Lyme disease, first identified in Lyme, Connecticut, is spread primarily by the deer tick, a tiny bloodsucker credited with carrying an illness that can do your Dane, and you, great physical harm! Borelliosis (the medical name of this disease) can affect your dog in several ways, but usually swelling and tenderness around the joints is observable. If you find a tick on your dog or suspect that the dog has been bitten by a tick, immediate veterinary care is advisable.

If you have been bitten by a tick or see the telltale tick bite with its characteristic surrounding of red (somewhat like a bull's-eye on a target), consult your physician or county health department. In both cases, yours and the dog's, timely diagnosis and treatment are essential.

Other Medical Conditions, Illnesses, and Concerns

Bloat (Gastric Tortion)

Bloat, or gastric tortion, is a very serious health concern for all large, deep-chested breeds of dogs, including the Great Dane. Bloat, which can painfully kill otherwise healthy dogs in just a few hours, involves a swelling and tortion of the dog's stomach from gas or water, or both. Bloat remains somewhat of a mystery, with a wide variety of suggested causes that may work independently of one another or in combination. Some of these are:
• A large meal followed by a large intake of water and strenuous exercise.
• A genetic predisposition in some breeds and even within some families in some breeds.
• Stress, brought about by many things.
• The sex and age of the dog appear to be factors. Males seem to be affected more often than females, and dogs over 24 months are more susceptible than younger animals.

Regardless of the causes, bloat remains a real killer of large dogs. Some clinical signs of bloat are:
• Obvious abdominal pain and noticeable abdominal swelling.
• Excessive salivation and rapid breathing.
• Pale and cool-to-the-touch skin in the mouth.
• A dazed and "shocky" look.

- Multiple attempts to vomit, especially when nothing comes up.

A dog with bloat needs immediate care if it is to stand a chance of survival. Don't panic. First, call your veterinarian, then safely transport your Dane *immediately* to the clinic.

Hip Dysplasia

Hip dysplasia, or HD, is another major canine health problem. While it does not have the usually fatal consequences of gastric tortion, it can be quite painful and debilitating. HD is a medical condition in which the hip joint is slack or loose, in combination with a deformity of the socket of the hip and the femoral head joining the thighbone. Malformed development of the hip's connecting tissues leaves an instable hip joint. Instead of being a stable receptacle, fitting like a cup for the end of the thighbone, the HD-affected hip socket is usually quite shallow. HD can cause a wobbling, unsteady gait that can be very painful to the dog.

HD is possibly inherited, but it must be acknowledged that not every puppy produced by dysplastic parents will have HD. It is also true that some nondysplastic parents will produce some dysplastic puppies.

HD cannot always be discovered until a puppy is older. The Orthopedic Foundation for Animals (OFA) has developed a widely used X-ray method of determining the presence or absence of HD. You should get a Great Dane puppy from a mating in which both parents have been tested and found free of this condition. This can reduce the chances of your pup's having this painful malady.

Diarrhea and Vomiting

Some diarrhea and vomiting can have ordinary causes like changes in food or added stress. In puppies, vomiting and diarrhea can also commonly result from internal parasites.

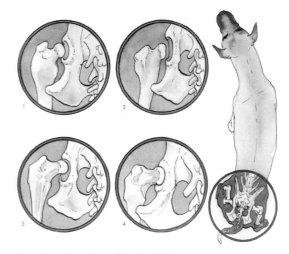

A visual explanation of hip dysplasia:
1. Acetabulum (socket) is shallow, definite subluxation (partial dislocation) is present;
2. Luxation (dislocation) is present—head of the femur is flattened;
3. Some partial dislocation (subluxation) is present in what could be a milder case;
4. Normal hip with good socket, no apparent subluxation.

Even so, both diarrhea and vomiting may be early warning signals of more serious ailments.

Any extended period (more than 12 to 24 hours) of vomiting or diarrhea should alert you to the need for a quick trip to the veterinarian. Even if this early alarm is a false one, the next one may not be.

Anal Sac Impaction

The anal glands lie just under the skin on each side of the anus. Normally these sacs are emptied naturally when the dog defecates. When they become stopped up or impacted, they must be emptied of their strong-smelling secretions by hand. One sign of impacted anal sacs is given when a dog scoots along the floor, dragging its rear end. The anal sacs can be emptied by your veterinarian. Alternatively, you can easily learn to do this yourself.

Inherited Conditions

Almost every breed of dog has one or more conditions that are passed along genetically from generation to generation. A tendency toward bloat and hip dysplasia are examples of such inherited conditions. When purchasing a young Great Dane, you should be aware of any health problems within the line. Avoid a Dane that comes from stock with the more serious problems that repeatedly occur in following generations. Cardiomyopathy, cervical spondylopathy (wobbler syndrome), and bone cancer are conditions that you should discuss with your veterinarian and Dane-breeder friends when evaluating any Great Dane for possible purchase.

Parasites

Internal Parasites

Dogs and puppies often have worms. Worms are parasites that draw their sustenance from your pet, and they can lead to serious health problems. Through simple tests, your veterinarian can detect the presence of worms, and he or she can also prescribe an appropriate drug treatment and eradication program. Even though various over-the-counter worm treatments are available, your dog's doctor knows how to treat your pet for these parasites in the most effective and safest manner.

Regular checkups will spot most parasites, but if you suspect that your Great Dane is being bothered by a parasitic infestation, don't wait for the next regular visit. The sooner your veterinarian confirms your suspicions and starts treatment, the better for your dog.

Worms are usually discovered by examination of your dog's stools or blood. The most common worms affecting dogs are roundworms, hookworms, tapeworms, and heartworms. Each of these parasites must be dealt with in its own specific way, and treatment is best handled by your veterinarian.

Roundworms: Even though dogs of all ages can have roundworm infestations, puppies are the most common target. Puppies often get roundworms even before they are born, since an infected mother dog can pass these parasites along to her offspring prenatally.

Roundworms are like weights pulling down a puppy's vitality, and pups with roundworms will not thrive. Roundworms take away the sharp and shiny look that a healthy puppy should have. A pendulous abdomen or potbelly may look cute on a puppy, but it is also a possible indication of roundworms. Puppies with roundworms may pass some of them in their stool or when they vomit. Recognize that roundworms sap the vim and vigor and the overall health of your Dane puppy and reduce its growth rate. If you discover roundworms, don't delay; get your puppy into a veterinarian's care to rid it of the health-robbing interlopers.

Another thing you can do to prevent roundworm infestation is to practice good kennel hygiene. Keep the puppy's area extremely clean and sanitary. Be especially vigilant in quickly and appropriately disposing of stools.

Hookworms: Another uninvited internal pest that can strike at dogs of any age, but really hurts puppies, is the hookworm. Puppies with hookworms can have bloody or tarlike stools and can also fail to thrive. Hookworm-infested puppies don't eat properly and fail to keep their weight.

Since hookworms are actually tiny vampires that attach themselves to the insides of the small intestines and suck blood, they can rapidly reduce a puppy to a greatly weakened state. A sometimes fatal consequence of hookworms in puppies is anemia.

Giant dogs have giant medical problems. Learn how to keep your pet healthy.

Your veterinarian knows how to handle these little bloodsuckers and how to put your puppy on the road to healthy adulthood. Kennel hygiene is a definite part of a successful treatment plan. Get rid of stools as soon as possible!

Tapeworms: Fleas are the common host of tapeworms, and they can share these parasites with your dog. Though they rarely debilitate a dog severely, these flat, segmented parasites impair your dog's health. A dog with tapeworms cannot be at its best. If you care for your Great Dane and want to see it grow into its full potential, then tapeworms are your adversary. Eliminating tapeworms from your dog will give it the vitality to remain healthy.

Consult your veterinarian about a treatment plan for the elimination of tapeworms. Also ask how to do away with the parasite that brought its own parasite to your pet—the flea. The elimination of a recurrent tapeworm infestation is another good reason to banish fleas from your dog's life.

Heartworms: Another parasite of a parasite, the heartworm, comes to your pet from its transport or intermediate host, the mosquito. A heartworm-infected mosquito bites your dog and deposits heartworm larvae on your pet's skin. The larvae enter the bloodstream through the hole made by the mosquito and ultimately travel to the heart.

Heartworm-larvae-infected mosquitoes are ready to share their ever-present threat in an ever-expanding portion of this country, and the disease now is present in most areas. Left untreated, heartworms cause heart failure and premature death.

Your veterinarian can help you with a plan to prevent heartworm infection. It involves regular testing and administration of medicine to kill heartworm larvae in circulation before they enter the heart. The medicine, however, is effective only in a dog that does not have an infection.

Fleas can be infested with a parasite themselves—the tapeworm that is passed on to your pet when the Dane swallows a flea. Another reason to keep fleas off your dog!

Treatment for heartworms is a long, risky, expensive procedure. Prevention—by far the better course of action—could save your Great Dane from an early and miserable death.

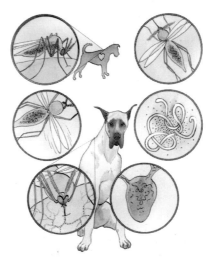

Mosquitoes pass on heartworm larva from other animals already infected with heartworms. Untreated, these larvae grow and can nearly clog a dog's heart, causing a lot of suffering and eventual death.

73

External Parasites

Fleas: Fleas are the bane of many a dog's life. They are the most common external parasite afflicting dogs, and they feed on your Great Dane's blood. In extreme cases, fleas can cause anemia in your dog; in almost all cases, they will make its life miserable. Fleas add insult to injury. Not only are they external parasites, but they also harbor internal parasites—tapeworms—and introduce them into your dog. Some dogs, like some humans, can have an extreme allergic reaction to flea bites. Flea-bite allergy makes its victim suffer far more than a nonallergic dog. This allergy can cause hair loss, skin infections, and incessant scratching. Immediate attention by a veterinarian and diligent flea control by the owner are required to alleviate this extremely uncomfortable condition.

Dealing with fleas involves a "take charge and take no prisoners" mentality. The sooner you realize that it is an all-out war between you and the fleas, the sooner you can begin to attack these little parasites in every place they live. If your dog has fleas, *every* place the dog goes will have fleas—its bed, the yard, the kennel, the car, and your home.

Failure to defeat your enemy in any one of these battlefields (and probably several others that you can name) is tantamount to complete failure. If fleas can survive in the yard, merely getting them out of the house is only a temporary victory; they will be back indoors in no time.

By consulting with your veterinarian and perhaps with a friend in the pet supply business, you should be able to obtain a variety of weapons for your flea war. Flea dips, flea shampoos, flea powder, flea collars, and flea spray are on-dog remedies. Their use should be coordinated by a call to your veterinarian and based on the knowledge that fleas spend 90 percent of their life cycle *off* your dog. Only the adult fleas, about 10 percent of the flea population, are on your dog.

To take care of the 90 percent that inhabit your yard, your car, your couch, and so forth, you must use other products. Ask your exterminator how to handle fleas off the dog. Always use flea killers with great care and follow the manufacturer's directions implicitly!

Ticks: The tick is another external parasite that can make a dog's life uncomfortable. Like fleas, ticks feed on the host's blood. Because ticks are much larger than fleas, they suck more blood and can increase their size by several hundred percent—all at the expense of your dog.

Not only are ticks a nuisance, they also carry a life-threatening disease (see Lyme Disease, page 70). If removed incorrectly, they can also cause infected sores and scars on your Dane. Not only are these sores painful, but because of the Great Dane's short coat they are unsightly as well.

Ticks can be controlled by the regular use of veterinarian-recommended on-dog sprays or dips and by living-area treatments. Never pull a tick off your Dane. Doing so may leave part of the tick's mouth parts in your dog's skin, which can lead to infection. To remove ticks, follow these steps:

• Place a small amount of rubbing alcohol at the exact site of the tick bite. Make sure that the dog doesn't get alcohol into its mouth or eyes!

• After making certain that the pet will remain still, use tweezers to grab the tick as close to the dog's skin as possible, pulling *very* slowly on the tick's head and mouth.

• Be certain to get all of the tick out of your Dane's skin, and then put additional alcohol or another antiseptic on the bite.

• Dispose of the tick properly, so that it will not get back on your dog or onto you!

- Sometimes you will see *two* ticks at one bite site, a large, blood-engorged one (the female) and a small, often dark brown one (the male). Be sure to get all of *both* ticks out of your Dane's skin.

Ticks like to get into a Dane's large, inviting ears. Always inspect your dog carefully after trips to the woods or to a park where ticks might be found and even after outings in the backyard.

Ear mites: The prominent ears (trimmed or untrimmed) of your Great Dane can be targets of another bothersome pest, the ear mite. These microscopic mites live in both the ear and the ear canal. Their presence can cause a dark, dirty, waxy material to adhere to the inner skin of the ears. Ear mites can cause dogs a great deal of discomfort, as evidenced by excessive ear scratching, or violent head-shaking.

Your Dane's veterinarian is your best line of defense against this parasitic invader. Regularly inspect your dog's ears. If you suspect ear mites, seek professional help to combat these pests, which are usually transmitted through contact with infected animals.

Mange: There are two types of mange, both caused by another form of mite:

- Red, or demodectic, mange especially affects physically vulnerable pets, like young puppies or oldsters, with ragged, patchy hair loss sometimes accompanied by severe itching.
- Sarcoptic mange (also known as scabies) comes from a type of mite that burrows into the dog's outer layers of skin. Scabies causes a great deal of hair loss and intense itching. This kind of mange doesn't confine itself to pets; it can also be transmitted to pet owners!

Both types can make your Dane uncomfortable, unsightly, and unhealthy. Let your veterinarian provide a treatment and eradication program.

Other Skin Problems

Great Danes may develop other skin problems, caused by fungi, allergies, or stress. Even the color of your Dane may partially account for these conditions. Blue dogs, in other breeds as well as in Danes, are more predisposed to skin problems than their fawn or brindle peers. Some pet foods have been known to incite rashes or "hot spots" in dogs.

You can avoid some skin problems by wisely choosing where you will buy your Great Dane. Good housekeeping and regular attention to your pet's coat can help control problems and parasites. Conferring with your veterinarian, not only after the fact, but ahead of time, will make skin problems less likely.

Emergency Care for Your Dane

The Team Approach

You will also need an emergency team to help you if an injury or an immobilizing sickness befalls your pet. Because of the sheer size of a Great Dane, you may want to line up help from your sturdier neighbors. In small towns you may be able to get someone from the police, fire, or sheriff's departments to give you a hand in getting your giant dog to medical care.

One Dane owner, herself not the largest of physical specimens, got several strapping lads from the local high school football team to help her. Another, equipped with an emergency-type gurney, slid an older, almost comatose Dane onto a blanket and then onto the gurney for transport to the owner's station wagon.

Some veterinarians make house-calls, but in an emergency this may not be possible. Always ask your veterinarian what to do when transporting a sick or injured dog. Because veterinarians deal with such issues all the time, they may have options and alternatives unknown to you.

HOW-TO:
Helping an Injured Pet

- Speak in a calm, reassuring voice; your hurt and frightened dog will pick up on any hysteria in your voice or demeanor.
- Always approach an injured animal slowly and deliberately, even if you have been friends with it for years. Speed is important, but if you are bitten, this will slow down the emergency-aid process.
- Gently, but securely, muzzle the dog (a Dane-sized muzzle might be a good addition to the first-aid kit). If no regular muzzle is available, use a necktie, belt, leash, or similar article.
- Attend to any immediate bleeding (see Bleeding, page 77) in an appropriate manner.
- If a helper with sufficient muscle power is available, put the dog on a makeshift stretcher such as a tabletop, a sturdy

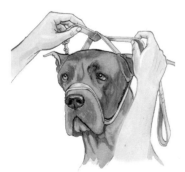

Making a muzzle out of a lead, a belt, or a necktie may keep an injured Dane from hurting itself further or injuring someone else.

piece of plywood, or even a strong tarpaulin. A third person, if available, should place both hands on the dog as the stretcher is lifted, securing the dog so it won't fall or jump off.
- If you have no helper, you'll need to devise a way to transport an injured pet to your vehicle. Some experts suggest tenderly placing the dog on a blanket or tarp, then sliding it to your car as gently as possible.
- Call your veterinarian to announce that you are on your way and will need help getting into the clinic.

Great Danes and other dogs of the giant breeds may require special care if they become seriously ill or injured. A responsible Dane owner will have an emergency plan worked out well in advance.

Accidents

In even the best of dog-owner relationships, where much preventive care and dog-proofing have taken place, accidents do happen. Be prepared for them.

The first rule in dealing with an injured canine: *Don't make things worse!* Rough handling can turn a simple fracture into a compound fracture, an injured back into paralysis, or a careless owner into an accident victim. As you assess the injury to your pet, try to keep a clear head. The dog may mean the world to you, but if you want to help your pet, you must act rationally.

Most serious injuries to pets, even huge Great Danes, occur when these canines are hit by a car. Do not allow your dog to run free, and be especially alert in situations where your dog could run out into a busy street or highway.

In rural areas, it is equally important to prevent accidents by keeping the Dane at home. A large fawn Great Dane looks astonishingly like a deer, and during hunting season such a dog could be killed by a hunter in a case of mistaken identity.

Heatstroke

Your Great Dane pet can die in a matter of minutes if left in an automobile with poor ventilation, where high temperatures can develop quickly on a sunny day, even when the weather is only moderately warm—60° Fahrenheit (15°C). A dog can die from heatstroke in an oven-hot car even if the windows are partially down. *Never* put your dog in such a dangerous, potentially fatal situation!

Clinical signs of heatstroke include a dazed look and rapid, shallow panting with a high fever. The dog's gums appear bright red. Speed is of the essence. Act *immediately*, even before going to the nearest veterinarian. Lower the dog's temperature by pouring cool water or a mixture of cool

Just getting a sick or injured giant dog to the veterinarian may not be an easy task. Plan ahead.

water and alcohol over its body, then go to the animal hospital.

Bleeding

If your Great Dane is bleeding, identify the source of the blood and apply firm but gentle pressure to the area with your hand. If the injury is on an extremity, place a tourniquet between the wound and the heart; loosen it for 30 to 60 seconds every 15 minutes. Continued bleeding, any significant blood loss, or a gaping wound require veterinary attention. Treat any bleeding as a serious situation worthy of your immediate attention!

Poisoning

Your Great Dane is at risk in a number of ways, but never more so than from accidental poisoning in its own home and yard. Because we live in a chemical-laden environment, there are any number of toxic materials that your pet could accidentally ingest. Some of the most dangerous and lethal poisons are products that we have around the house and use every day.

The Life Span of the Great Dane

Giant dogs do not have correspondingly long life spans. Sadly, a Great Dane is often an old dog when members of toy or other smaller breeds are just entering middle age. Your Dane, on average, will not live much past eight years of age. You and your family must face this reality when you decide to make a Great Dane a member of your family. Some Danes live longer than that, while others have even shorter natural lives. You can improve the odds by choosing a Great Dane from a line or pedigreed family that tends to be longer lived.

Old Age and Your Great Dane

When the inquisitive youngster, all legs and ears, becomes the distinguished, gray-muzzled veteran, your treatment of your pet Dane must change. The old Dane will sleep a little more, and its play will be a little less vigorous. The oldster will still love its family and want to be included, but it can't go as fast as before.

A new set of issues will be important now. Your Dane may need a dog food for senior canines. Its teeth and gums will need extra care. There may be some hearing loss and possible eye problems. Most of these issues can be handled by timely visits to the veterinarian and by attention to the changing needs of your pet.

Areas Needing Your Ongoing Attention

Teeth

Your Great Dane needs good dental care all its life. Tartar accumulation can bring on gum and tooth disease. You can lessen tartar and also ensure good dental health for your dog by:
• Regularly inspecting your Great Dane's teeth and gums, not only for tartar, but also for signs of tooth decay and foreign objects (such as pieces of wood from the dog's chewing on sticks);
• Cleaning your Great Dane's teeth at home;
• Scheduling regular veterinary dental checkups, with occasional professional teeth cleaning to supplement your efforts;
• Using veterinarian-approved chew toys and dental exercisers, designed to help remove tartar and plaque.

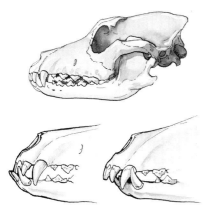

Normal Dane skull (top); a skull showing an underbite (bottom, left); a skull showing an overbite (bottom, right). Underbites and overbites are definite defects in Great Danes.

Eyes

The large, prominent eyes of the Great Dane will need some attention from you as the dog ages. Other than the puppy-proofing and Dane-proofing that should be a part of your regular regimen, you need to protect your dog from sharp objects at eye level. You also need to keep the Dane safe from toxic substances or fumes that can irritate or damage its eyes.

Neighborhood children, by throwing stones or shooting an air rifle at what is probably the biggest dog in the neighborhood, can harm your Dane. Air pollution, thorny plants, and heavy underbrush all have eye-damaging potential. Aging can bring on problems like cataracts. All of these eye problems can be considerably lessened in severity if regular eye inspections are done by you and by your veterinarian during general checkups.

You may notice mucus collected in the corners of your Great Dane's eyes from time to time. This is usually a perfectly normal condition, and the matter can be removed by gentle wiping with a soft cloth. Don't, however, confuse this ordinary mucus-like material with an eye discharge, which can signal an eye problem that needs professional attention.

Ears

The ears of a Great Dane are among its most striking features. Whether your Dane's ears have been cropped like those of many show dogs or remain in their natural, unclipped state, they need your regular attention and ongoing care. Dog ears are among the favorite hiding places of parasites like ticks and ear mites (see Ticks, page 74, and Ear mites, page 75). Regular inspection of the ears will let you spot these little invaders early and begin to get rid of them.

Sometimes a male dog's ears are a record of its hostile interactions with other male dogs. Because of their location—high up on either side of the dog's head—ears also suffer damage when a big, fast dog runs through underbrush. Keep a close watch on

A Great Dane will need regular veterinary check-ups all its life if it is to be at its best.

your pet's ears for cuts or scratches that may need medical attention, yours or the veterinarian's.

Feet and Nails

Although the feet of every dog are healthier if its owner gives them regular care, the feet of a huge dog, which often support a weight of over 150 pounds (68 kg), absolutely must have good owner care. One owner of a large brindle male asserted, "If you don't think that the feet of a Great Dane take a lot of punishment, let my dog step on your foot with just one of his."

A small dog may be able to get around on a bad foot or a foot with an injured toenail, but giant dogs have considerably more trouble when their running gear is in poor condition. Good nail care needs to start when the Great Dane is a puppy, and it has to include preventive maintenance and an effort to keep broken glass and other foot-harming items out of the dog's path. The care of a Dane's feet is as important as any other part of the dog's health plan.

Danes put great stress on their footpads and nails. Regular inspections will let you know if your dog has suffered a slight abrasion that could become a bigger foot problem later. Regular nail trimming is a must. You need a Dane-

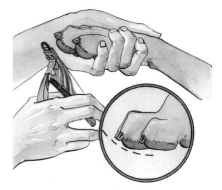

Keeping a Dane's nails trimmed using a guillotine-style nail trimmer. The inset shows the correct way to file the nails. This illustration also shows the "quick" or vein, which should be avoided in doing a "peticure" on your Great Dane.

worthy set of toenail clippers, either the scissors type or the "guillotine" type. Use them whenever the dog's nails start to grow too long. Remember to keep well away from the "quick," or the main blood supply, of the nail. You may have to use an emery board or nail file to shorten nails when the "quick" is too close for easy trimming.

Giving Your Dane Medicine

You should know how to give your Great Dane the medicines for treatment or prevention prescribed by the dog's veterinarian. Some dogs don't like to take medicine and spit out pills and capsules. Some experienced owners hide the pill or capsule in a dog treat—bread spread with canned dog food, for example—or in a little clump of semimoist food.

Others take the more direct approach of opening the dog's mouth, slightly tilting its head back, and placing the pill as far back on the dog's tongue as they can reach. Then they close the dog's mouth, speak calmingly, and wait for the dog to swallow.

Liquid medicine is administered in a similar way. Remembering to keep the head tilted only slightly, pour the medicine over the back of the tongue. Speak soothingly as you close the Dane's mouth and wait for the dog to swallow.

Always follow the veterinarian's dosages and instructions carefully. Never use outdated medicines or give your Great Dane medication designed for humans or other animals without prior approval from your dog's veterinarian.

Euthanasia

That gangling puppy you chose will grow to become a majestic Great Dane and a full member of your family. Just as certainly, barring premature death from illness or accident, this majestic friend will grow to be an old Dane. In the best of all possible worlds, every good old dog would live

When you choose a Dane puppy, try to see its mother (dam) and father (sire) if at all possible.

a full, healthy life and die painlessly in its sleep one night. In the real world, things don't always work out that way.

Great Danes have much good fortune. Their beauty and regal strength are admired by Dane breeders and others the world over. When the Dane grows old, however, its size tends to work against it. That great height and weight can become a burden for an old dog. For some Danes, the ravages of old age bring pain and discomfort to their last years.

Your Great Dane, I hope, will close its life in the easiest way possible, with never a painful day. If that does not occur, however, and your old friend begins to suffer, a difficult choice has to be made. When living becomes unbearable for your pet, take your veterinarian's counsel and give serious consideration to ending the dog's suffering. Such a decision is never easy, but a gentle, painless, humane end is far better for the dog than incessant, acute discomfort.

Raising Great Danes

Should You Breed Your Dane?

If you are a novice dog breeder, the answer is almost certainly *"No!"* Producing more dogs is irresponsible when thousands of dogs are killed each day, not because they aren't healthy or wouldn't make good pets, but because there aren't enough homes for them. The only legitimate reason to breed dogs is to improve the breed.

A Hard, Realistic Look

Before you decide that raising Great Danes is an activity you want to pursue, you should recognize that allowing more Great Danes to be born is not something to be decided quickly or without appropriate forethought. A responsible dog breeder makes certain that each and every puppy in a litter will have a good home.

If a puppy's new home doesn't work out, most responsible breeders want the dog back in order to locate another home. A puppy that can't be placed may very well remain with the breeder as a pet for the remainder of its life!

Imagine that you breed your Great Dane female, and she has eight healthy puppies. You keep one pup for yourself and find good homes for four others. Because good homes for giant dogs are not easy to find, you are left with three additional puppies (in addition to your mother dog and the one you chose to keep) to care for, feed, house, and love. Although you may eventually be able to place an older puppy or an adult in a suitable environment, you may end up with five Great Danes.

Every puppy you raise deserves a good home. If you can't find that home elsewhere, you will have to keep the dog in your own home. Unless you are willing to keep several large dogs for their entire lives, don't consider attempting to breed Great Danes.

Why Breed for Pet Quality?

Even the most carefully planned Great Dane mating, between a top-quality female and the best stud dog imaginable, will probably produce more pet-quality puppies than puppies with genuine show or breeding poten-

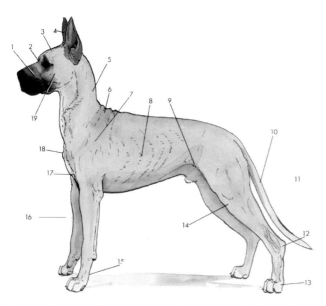

Parts of the Great Dane: 1. muzzle 2. stop 3. skull 4. ear 5. neckline 6. withers 7. shoulder 8. rib cage 9. loin 10. tail 11. hindquarters 12. hock 13. rear pastern 14. stifle 15. front pastern 16. forequarters 17. brisket 18. chest 19. cheek

tial. That is *doubly* true of breeding harlequins! Since the pets far outnumber the show prospects, deliberately setting out to produce pet pups by breeding your pet-quality Dane to someone else's pet-quality Dane is both unwise and irresponsible.

The only legitimate reason to breed a Great Dane is to produce the best possible offspring. If your female lacks the requisite genetic potential, have her spayed and let her become the best possible pet. Don't add to an already overabundant supply of unwanted puppies. If you want another puppy as a companion for your female or as a replacement when she is gone, buy it, don't breed to obtain it! You will spend less to buy a top-quality show prospect or obedience puppy than to arrange for a litter to be born, pay all the related costs, and keep all the unplaced pups.

If you answer these questions (below) honestly and decide that you want to raise Great Danes, you face a task of no small proportions. Apprentice yourself to an experienced and wiser Dane breeder who can serve as a mentor or adviser in this endeavor.

Seek out someone who is respected both as a Dane breeder and as a person, and then follow his or her guidance. Join the Great Dane Club of America (see Useful Addresses, page 92) and your local breed clubs. Be an active, helpful, and useful member; you will gain in your knowledge of Great Danes and in your stature as a potential breeder of Danes.

Color Breeding Guidelines

In some breeds it matters little what colors are bred together but that is certainly *not* true of Great Danes. Regardless of whether you have chosen blacks or fawns, blues or brindles, they, like the harlequins, have specific color breeding conditions that you need to know and follow. The Great Dane Club of America recognizes those five colors and sets forth guidelines to prevent inappropriate mixed color breedings. Such breedings result in the birth of more and more puppies that are unacceptable for breeding or showing.

Some Questions for You to Consider

Before you make up your mind to become a Dane breeder, ask yourself some basic questions:

1. Am I willing to spend what it will take to get the best available Great Dane with which to start?

2. Do I and my family have the resources, financial and other, to embark on this admittedly risky endeavor, and is the entire family as committed to it as I am?

3. Am I willing to search diligently for good homes for all the puppies I raise and to maintain a lifelong interest in all of them?

4. If I must keep several unplaced pups, do I have enough space and time to give each Great Dane the room and attention it needs to thrive?

5. Do I realize that dog raising is not a lucrative undertaking and that most dog breeders spend far more than they ever earn with dogs?

6. Is my goal to produce the best possible Great Danes? Am I willing to see that promising pups get dog show exposure, and am I willing to accept the opinion of judges and other breeders if it turns out to be negative?

7. Am I willing to study the Great Dane standard, other reference materials, and pedigrees and to listen to more experienced breeders, in order to become a competent Great Dane breeder?

You can get a copy of these guidelines, called the "Breeders Code Of Ethics," from the Great Dane Club of America. Essentially they are as follows:

1. Fawn dogs should be bred only to fawn and brindle dogs.
2. Brindle dogs should be bred only to brindle or fawn dogs.
3. Blue Danes should be bred only to blues, pure blacks, or blacks of blue parentage.
4. Black Great Danes (of pure black parentage) should be bred to other pure blacks, to blues, or to harlequins.
5. Harlequins should be bred only to harlequins, pure blacks, or blacks from harlequin breedings.

Remember that there are three kinds of black Danes: Danes from exclusively black genetic heritage, which I have called "pure blacks"; blacks from matings where one parent was a blue Dane; and blacks, often with the "Boston" color pattern, from harlequin matings. The pure black is the only one that can be used interchangeably. The blue-bred blacks should stay with blue breedings, and the harlequin-bred blacks should stay with that color pattern. Most Dane breeders discourage mating blacks or blues with fawns or brindles; virtually all breeders discourage mating fawns, brindles, or blues with harlequins.

Each Great Dane puppy deserves a good and loving home.

Should You Breed Your Harlequin?

Low probability of success: Everything that can go wrong for a novice Dane breeder of the other colors is doubly risky for the novice who wants to raise harlequins. This color pattern is probably the most difficult of all to breed. Not only do you need extremely good luck, even when top specimens are mated, but the numerical odds are against even the best and most experienced breeder's producing more than one or two show prospect harlequins in each litter.

Leave it to the experts: A litter of eight puppies from the best male and female harlequins in the world may include poorly colored harlequins, "Boston" colored or "mantled" blacks. Owning a beautiful harlequin Great Dane can be a great experience, but raising harlequins may not be so great. Unless you have a burning desire to become a serious harlequin Dane breeder, you are well advised to leave harlequins to the experts. Of course, in a few years you may be ready to try breeding this beautiful and difficult color.

The Breeding Female

Condition, Temperament, Quality

Without three key elements, your Great Dane bitch may not be a good candidate for breeding:

Condition: Unless your female is in good physical shape, she probably is a poor choice to mother a litter of Great Dane puppies. Her genetic background should be free of apparent (or suspected) inherited health problems that might be passed on to her offspring.

Her health history is also important. If she was not properly cared for as a puppy and lacked a healthy start, she probably shouldn't be used for breeding. While some dogs have recovered from near starvation or severe abuse, breeding such a female in the hope of obtaining an optimally healthy litter is a definite gamble.

Your female's current health is important. Has she just recovered from some illness that might have left her in a weakened state or might have a negative effect on any puppies she might bear? Breeding a bitch not in top shape is never a good idea. It is risky for the bitch and could result in a poor-quality litter.

Temperament: Unless your Great Dane female is of sound temperament, there is absolutely no reason to breed from her. Any puppies she might produce would always be suspect. A Great Dane without a good disposition is always a potential liability and definitely not a breeding prospect.

Quality: As I explained elsewhere (see Pet Quality or Show Quality, page 40), quality has nothing to do with your female's virtues as a pet. If her health and temperament are sound, the acid test of her fitness to produce more Great Danes is her quality in terms of the Great Dane breed standard formulated for judging show dogs. Generally, unless your Dane bitch herself is of show quality,

Since merles are not considered breeding stock, they should be spayed or neutered.

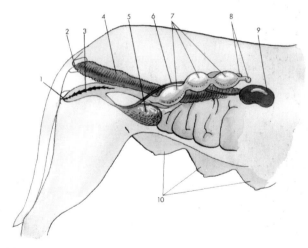

The reproductive system of the female Great Dane: 1. vulva 2. anus 3. vagina 4. rectum 5. bladder 6. ureter 7. developing embryos 8. ovaries 9. kidneys 10. mammary glands

she should not be considered a potential brood dam for show puppies. There are exceptions to every situation (as with the "Boston"-colored dogs of otherwise excellent quality that are sometimes bred with harlequins), but they are uncommon.

The best test of quality for your female is to enter her in competition in an AKC dog show. If she does well, you may have an affirmative answer and a possible show career for her before she becomes a breeding female. If she does not do well, you may also have an answer. You might also ask your Dane mentor about her potential.

The Breeding Male

Condition, Temperament, Quality, Compatibility

Similarly to a Great Dane female, a male Dane does not automatically qualify to become a breeding male or stud

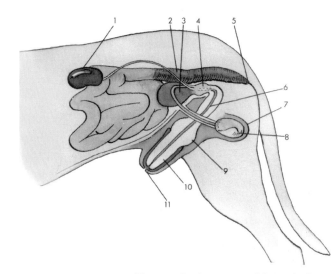

The reproductive system of the male Great Dane: 1. kidneys 2. rectum 3. bladder 4. prostate 5. anus 6. urethra 7. scrotum 8. testes 9. bulb 10. penis 11. sheath

dog. To be a potential stud dog, your male must meet certain requirements:

Condition: Like a breeding female, a male must be free of inherited health problems, previous health problems, and current health problems. A stud dog will be no credit to the future of the breed if his puppies are shackled with genetic problems, nor will he be much of a producer if his own background has been one of neglect and deprivation. Additionally, a Great Dane male that is in poor physical condition may be unable to mate, may not produce a viable litter if he does mate, and may negatively affect the health of any offspring.

Temperament: The best Great Dane male in the world should be deemed unfit for breeding if it is an overly aggressive, vicious dog. Not only is such a dog a danger in his own right, but he may well pass along his bad disposition to his offspring, thus perpetuating a trait that the early Dane breeders (and all responsible Great Dane breeders since) wanted to eliminate from the breed.

Quality: Unless a Great Dane male has truly exceptional quality, usually attested by an AKC Champion title before his name, his worth as a stud dog is minimal. There are a great many Dane males; why should any but the very best be chosen to produce the Danes of tomorrow? Expert dog breeders look for more than excellence in the stud dog himself. The better studs are those which, when mated to quality females, sire offspring that are as good as they and the mothers are. The best stud dogs, called "prepotent" studs, produce puppies better than their mothers and sometimes even better than both parents! This last type, rare in any breed, comes along maybe once in a generation—a human generation!

Compatibility: Unless the stud dog has a pedigree compatible with that of the breeding female, the chances for a litter of top-quality puppies are greatly reduced. When choosing a stud dog for your female, depend on the advice of more experienced Dane fanciers, study pedigrees, and then breed to the very best stud that meets your requirements, regardless of cost.

Breeding your Great Dane female to a top male may be an expensive arrangement, though stud fees vary. Sometimes the male's owner is willing to take a pick-of-the-litter puppy as full or partial payment. This is the male's owner's pick, not yours. The stud owner may also require a written certificate from your veterinarian, stating that your female has no obvious congenital or physical conditions that disqualify her as a brood (breeding) bitch and that she is free of the venereally transmitted bacterial disease called brucellosis. Brucellosis is incurable, and it can be transmitted to humans. It can do great harm to breeding dogs, sometimes causing aborted litters or even sterility in the breeding adults.

A stud dog's owner will want to be certain that a breeding to your Dane bitch will not harm his or her stud. The owner is concerned not only about physical harm, including brucellosis, but also about the possible damage to the stud's reputation if the litter contains several genetically deformed puppies or if the overall quality of the progeny is poor. The better the pups sired by a stud dog, the more demand there is likely to be for that dog. The better the females bred to any male, the greater the chance of that male to sire superior puppies, perhaps even that one great puppy every responsible breeder seeks.

The stud's owner should offer you a guarantee that the mating will result in conception and, ultimately, in live puppies. If conception does not take place, normally the stud's owner will allow a remating at your Dane's next heat. It is always wise to get this guarantee in writing—in advance.

When to Breed

Age

Your Great Dane female should be past puppyhood herself before she undergoes the rigors of bearing puppies. The fact that she comes into heat and is physically capable of being bred does not mean that she *should* be bred. It will take you time to assess her condition, temperament, and quality as an adult dog. No bitch should be bred until she is at least two years old and has received her OFA evaluation for hip dysplasia.

The Estrous Cycle

Your Great Dane female will generally come into heat, or season, two times each year. A bitch experiences her first heat at between six and eight months of age, but that may vary somewhat within breeds and within individual bitches. This periodic coming into season, called the estrous cycle, can have several stages:

Proestrus: This is the beginning of the cycle. Proestrus is identified by the onset of activity within the uterus and ovaries. The ovaries begin to produce eggs (ova). As these mature, the uterus wall becomes thicker, the vulva (the outer external genitalia) becomes enlarged, and a blood-tinged discharge from the bitch's vagina can be seen. Proestrus continues for about nine days, though in some cases it has been a short as four days and as long as 14. Males will be attracted to your Great Dane bitch during proestrus, but she will not be receptive to mating.

Estrus: The second phase of the cycle begins when the vaginal discharge loses some of its bloody tint and becomes clearer and thicker. Ovulation takes place during estrus, normally between the ninth and fourteenth days after the cycle began. Mating and conception are possible during this stage, which may last as long as nine days.

Only the very best Danes deserve to carry on the breed; and even then, there will always be more average puppies than great ones.

Metestrus: If your female mated and conceived in the early stage, her organs now begin to prepare for the birth of puppies. Metestrus signals the start of mammary growth and preparation for lactation (milk production).

Anestrus: This stage of the estrous cycle marks the end of metestrus and the end of the estrous cycle. The uterus and ovaries begin to resume their pre-heat appearance.

If your Great Dane bitch has not mated and has not conceived, her organs will gradually return to normal. Vaginal discharge will cease, and her ovaries will go into a phase of inactivity ready to start the estrous cycle all over again in about six months.

Tip: During the entire estrous cycle, you would be wise to keep your female away from breeding-age males (including older puppies). Otherwise, you could have an unwanted pregnancy to deal with. Keep your Dane bitch under control at all times. If a male can mate with her during this cycle—and some males are amazing in their persistence and inventiveness—she could get pregnant.

Mating

Dog breeders generally introduce the stud dog to the bitch on the ninth day of the estrus (ovulating) stage of the estrous cycle. When mating, or copulating, the male and the female normally become "tied" or locked together as a result of changes in the vagina and the penis. This condition should last only a few minutes. If the stud and the bitch remain together, they may mate again during the approximately two days of the female's maximum receptiveness. It is important to know that your female could mate with another dog after being mated to the Great Dane stud. Safeguard her to keep this from happening. If your female is mated to another dog, the parentage of her pups will be in question. Keep a female in the estrus stage away from any unneutered male that you don't wish to have father her puppies!

Pregnancy

Gestation, or the period of time it takes for the puppies to arrive after mating, for dogs is normally 58 to 63 days. About six weeks following the mating, your Great Dane bitch will begin to take on a maternal appearance. Her abdomen will begin to get larger and her teats will swell.

Special Care

During this time, be especially gentle with her. If this is her first litter, she will need to be reassured that what is happening to her is all right. Most Dane breeders give a pregnant female a diet of good-quality puppy food during the last third of her pregnancy, but she needs to be gaining weight from growing puppies and not from overeating. Keep up moderate exercise until about two weeks before the due date.

At this time you would be wise to cut out any overly strenuous activity and separate her from other dogs or small children that might jostle or bump her. Extra attention and care are needed now. Keep her relaxed and as free from stress as possible.

The Whelping Box

You have known these puppies were coming for weeks now. Prepare for their birth well in advance. First, provide a good whelping box with ample room for the mother to turn around and to lie comfortably on her side. Since the box is not only a birthing place but also the puppies' home for the first few weeks, the mother needs sufficient room to stretch out and allow her litter to nurse.

Put the whelping box in a warm, dry place, away from drafts and foot traffic. Your Dane will need to feel that her babies are secure, and that is impossible if the whelping box is in a spot bustling with activity. (Note: Some mother Danes are quite protective of their new offspring, and a delivery person or neighbor could be in for a surprise if he or she blunders into the puppies' area.)

A contented mother Dane with her puppies in a well-constructed whelping box. The all-important shelf will keep a mother from unintentionally crushing one of her babies.

A Dane-sized whelping box should have sides high enough to keep a litter of young puppies from getting out. It also needs a shelf inside that will keep a puppy from getting crushed between its mother and the sides of the box. This is *important!*

Cover the floor of the whelping box with several layers of newspaper (use only black and white; avoid the pages with colored ink). As the puppies mess up the top layer of paper, lift it up, leaving the other layers in place. This helps keep the box clean without creating fuss for the newborns and their proud mother.

Preparing for the Puppies' Arrival

With the construction or purchase of a whelping box you have begun preparations for the big event. Most Great Danes have little trouble whelping, but you probably will want to be close by, especially if this is your female's first litter. Most expectant mother dogs become restless and need your gentle words and tender care. Sometimes Great Dane females become more sensitive than usual as birthing time nears. Make every allowance for your pet's condition, and be supportive by spending as much time with her as possible.

You should have primed yourself by discussing the whelping procedure with your veterinarian and your Dane mentors, or perhaps by reading on this subject in greater depth. Now is not the time to pretend you have knowledge or confidence that you lack. Seek assistance from experienced, trusted advisors, and follow their advice.

Your whelping kit may include the following items (and others that your advisors deem important):

• A heating pad and a temporary-care box for early arrivals.
• Heavy surgical thread and sharp scissors to cut and tie off umbilical cords.
• Clean, soft, absorbent towels to dry the newborns.
• A list of important phone numbers, including those of the veterinarian and your Dane mentor (who may sit with you if the Dane doesn't mind).

Whelping

Under normal circumstances, as the puppies begin to be born the mother dog pulls away the birth sac and chews through the umbilical cord of each pup. If she fails to do so, you may have to assist her. The mother normally licks each puppy clean and gently nudges it toward her teats for its first meal. If you assist her in any way, move slowly and speak quietly to avoid exciting her or diverting her attention from the next birth.

Each puppy should be followed by a certain amount of afterbirth, which the mother normally eats. If, after all the puppies are born, you suspect some afterbirth has not been expelled, call your veterinarian.

As the puppies are born, place each one into the heated box. Make sure the pad is set on "low" and covered by a towel, so that the box doesn't get too hot. That will keep the pups from becoming chilled until your Great Dane, now a mother, can assume full care of them.

Care of Older Puppies

You have helped give the newborn Danes a good start and the mother is probably taking excellent care of them, but your job is not done. Your mother Dane can only do so much to ensure that her offspring will survive. Many other things have to be done to give the pups the best chance not only to survive, but to begin developing into the giants of their genetic heritage.

During the first few weeks, keep the place where the puppies live in a temperature range of 80° to 90° Fahrenheit (27° to 32°C). Puppies simply cannot tolerate temperature extremes. While their mother's big, warm body will help keep them warm, you can be of real help in maintaining an environment within the safety zone.

As the puppies grow older they will be much less vulnerable to minor fluctuations in temperature. If you use an external source to maintain warmth, make sure that it is not too close to the puppies or within reach of inquisitive youngsters. Puppy-proofing begins here all over again. If a puppy should get out of the whelping box, make sure there is nothing nearby that can harm it.

Your mother dog will usually provide good care for the puppies during their first weeks of life. She will feed them, clean them, and clean up after them. Even before their eyes open, their mother has begun to provide lessons and support for her puppies. If for some reason your Great Dane bitch can't give her pups adequate care, this job will fall to you. You will have to feed them with veterinarian-approved milk replacer, and that is no simple task. Hungry Great Dane puppies with a lot of growing to do in a short time will need to be fed about every four hours during the first days and weeks of their lives. If you forget or are a little late, the loud whimpers and squeals of the baby Danes will remind you to get moving. One result of this hand-feeding experience is a uniquely close bonding between the pups and you, which can be a great aid in their early socialization.

When the puppies are about six weeks old, they will need their first temporary shots from your veterinarian. Worming checks and overall exams also can be done at this time. The puppies are still too young to leave their first home and their mama, but they are growing rapidly now, and you have other responsibilities to fill your time.

Weaning the pups at the right time is an important stage in their development. Gradually shifting the pups from sole dependence on their mother to solid food is another task you will have to perform. Feed a top-quality diet to get the youngsters started. Slowly introduce the puppies to moistened bits of dry food. Let them smell the aroma of the food and lick the new, good-tasting stuff off your fingers. Gradually introduce this food into their area, but not into their whelping box. You need to feed wet, but not soggy, dry food to them at first, gradually cutting back on the moisture in the food. Put the puppies' drinking water in another dish nearby.

Use a flat-bottomed pan to feed these now quite active pups. You want a food container that will allow the pups ready access to the food, but that will be hard to turn over. Thoroughly clean the food and water pans each day, and keep the area around the whelping box clean. This will help keep your pups healthy.

Tip: It is important that the puppies *not* have contact with dogs other than their mother and their littermates until they have received their vaccinations at 12 weeks. It is also important that the pups not be exposed to the fecal material, toys, or living areas of other adult dogs until the last of their immunizations is given at 16 to 18 weeks.

Socializing the Puppies

An important phase in the lives of these puppies is the socialization that begins as they are introduced to humans other than you, your family, and your veterinarian. Never underestimate the effect that this time in a young puppy's life may have in the years to come. The socialization process gives the puppies a chance to meet other humans, come to like them, and learn not to fear them. By performing this not at all unpleasant job, you give these Great Danes a start toward emotional stability that may prove crucial as they grow older. Some hints on socializing puppies:

Give individual attention: Be sure that each puppy gets time with you and other humans by itself, every day.

Be gentle: Roughhousing is inappropriate with these little pups. The accent is on gentle, nonthreatening, introductory actions.

Give a wide view: Choose a broad spectrum of socializers. Children do well (if supervised), but you want the puppies to get to know a wide variety of people at this key time. Men and women, older people and youngsters, people of different ethnic backgrounds— all should be used to give your puppies a wide view of humankind. Unless these puppies are going to be raised and live their entire lives in isolation from all humans other than you, you would be wise to introduce them to all kinds of people.

After a few more weeks these puppies will be ready for new homes. Your care of their mother, your aid at their births, your provision of a good environment, and your active attention to good socialization have paved the way for each of these little Great Danes to become a successful pet. You have invested heavily in these youngsters; now you want to find the best home possible for each of them!

Useful Addresses and Literature

International Kennel Clubs

Great Dane Club of America*
 Marie A. Fint
 442 Country View Lane
 Garland, Texas 75043

American Kennel Club
 51 Madison Avenue
 New York, New York 10038

Australian Kennel Club
 Royal Show Ground
 Ascot Vale
 Victoria, Australia

Canadian Kennel Club
 2150 Bloor Street
 Toronto, Ontario M6540

The Kennel Club
 1-4 Clargis Street, Picadilly
 London, W7Y 8AB
 England

New Zealand Kennel Club
 P.O. Box 523
 Wellington, 1
 New Zealand

Information and Printed Material

American Boarding Kennel
 Association
 4575 Galley Road, Suite 400 A
 Colorado Springs, Colorado
 80915
(Publishes lists of approved
boarding kennels.)

*This address may change with the
election of new club officers. The
current listing can be obtained by
contacting the American Kennel
Club.

American Society for the
 Prevention of Cruelty to
 Animals (ASPCA)
 441 East 92nd Street
 New York, New York 10128

American Veterinary Medical
 Association
 930 North Meacham Road
 Schaumberg, Illinois 60173

Gaines TWT
 P.O. Box 8172
 Kankakee, Illinois 60901
(Publishes *Touring with Towser*,
a directory of hotels and motels
that accommodate guests with
dogs.)

Humane Society of the United
States (HSUS)
 2100 L Street NW
 Washington, DC 20037

Books
In addition to the most recent edition of the official publication of the American Kennel Club, *The Complete Dog Book*, published by Howell Book House, New York, other suggestions include:

Alderton, David. *The Dog Care Manual*. Hauppauge, New York: Barron's Educational Series, Inc., 1986.

Baer, Ted. *Communicating with Your Dog*. Hauppauge, New York: Barron's Educational Series, Inc., 1989.

_____ . *How to Teach Your Old Dog New Tricks*. Hauppauge, New York: Barron's Educational Series, Inc., 1991.

Frye, Fredric. *First Aid for Your Dog*. Hauppauge, New York: Barron's Educational Series, Inc., 1987.

Klever, Ulrich. *The Complete Book of Dog Care*. Hauppauge, New York: Barron's Educational Series, Inc., 1989.

_____ . *Dogs: A Mini Fact Finder*. Hauppauge, New York: Barron's Educational Series, Inc., 1990.

Pinney, Chris C., *Guide to Home Pet Grooming*. Hauppauge, New York: Barron's Educational Series, Inc., 1990.

Ullmann, Hans. *The New Dog Handbook*. Hauppauge, New York: Barron's Educational Series, Inc., 1984.

Wrede, Barbara. *Civilizing Your Puppy*. Hauppauge, New York: Barron's Educational Series, Inc., 1992.

Magazines

The Dane Quarterly
 3518 El Camino Real #311
 Atascadero, CA 93422

The Great Dane Journal
 P.O. Box 4408
 Ocala, FL 34478

The Great Dane Reporter
 P.O. Box 150
 Riverside, CA 92502-0150

Index

Acknowledgment

The author wishes to thank Dr. Matt Vriends, Michele Earle-Bridges, Dr. Carol Himsel Daly, Don Reis, and Paul Royster for all of their efforts that turned a jumble of words into a dog book.

About the Author

Joe Stahlkuppe, a lifelong dog fancier and breeder, writes a column for a pet industry magazine and works as regional sales director for a major pet food manufacturer. He is also the author of Barron's *Pomeranians: A Complete Pet Owner's Manual* and *Keeshonden: A Complete Pet Owner's Manual.*

Photo Credits

Cathie Abbott: pages 4, 88
Gary W. Ellis: pages 9 (lower), 12 (upper), 23 (upper), 30 (lower), 31 (two), 37, 40, 45, 58 (upper), 63, 72, 81, 84
Susan Green: pages 5, 9 (upper), 18, 30 (upper), 44, 69
D. J. Hamer: front cover, back cover, pages 19 (left), 41
Jay Hulsey: pages 8 (lower), 85
Judith E. Strom: pages 19 (right), 22, 62, 65, 80
Bob and Kay Thompson: pages 16 (two), 58 (lower), 77
Wim van Vugt: inside front cover, inside back cover, pages 8 (upper), 12 (lower), 13 (two), 23 (lower), 36, 48

All inquiries should be addressed to
Barron's Educational Series, Inc.
250 Wireless Boulevard
Hauppauge, NY 11788

International Standard Book No.
0-8120-1418-9

Library of Congress Catalog Card No. 94-17552

Library of Congress Cataloging-in-Publication Data
Stahlkuppe, Joe.
    Great Danes : everything about purchase, care, nutrition, breeding, behavior, and training / Joe Stahlkuppe ; with drawings by Michele Earle-Bridges.
        p. cm.
    Includes index.
    ISBN 0-8120-1418-9
    1. Great Danes. I. Title.
SF429.G7S73   1994
636.7´3—dc20   94-17552
                                      CIP

PRINTED IN HONG KONG

45678   9927   987654321

Important Notes

This pet owner's guide tells the reader how to buy and care for a Great Dane. The author and the publisher consider it important to point out that the advice given in the book is meant primarily for normally developed puppies from a good breeder—that is, dogs of excellent physical health and good character.

Anyone who adopts a fully grown dog should be aware that the animal has already formed its basic impressions of human beings. The new owner should watch the animal carefully, including its behavior toward humans, and should meet the previous owner. If the dog comes from a shelter, it may be possible to get some information on the dog's background and peculiarities there. There are dogs that, as a result of bad experiences with humans, behave in an unnatural manner or may even bite. Only people that have experience with dogs should take in such animals.

Caution is further advised in the association of children with dogs, in meeting with other dogs, and in exercising the dog without a leash.

Even well-behaved and carefully supervised dogs sometimes do damage to someone else's property or cause accidents. It is therefore in the owner's interest to be adequately insured against such eventualities, and we strongly urge all dog owners to purchase a liability policy that covers their dog.

Perfect for Pet Owners!

3JOHNMOO179949

PET OWNER'S MANUALS

Over 50 illustrations per book (20 or more color photos), 72–80 pp., paperback.

AFRICAN GRAY PARROTS (3773-1)
AMAZON PARROTS (4035-X)
BANTAMS (3687-5)
BEAGLES (3829-0)
BEEKEEPING (4089-9)
BOSTON TERRIERS (1696-3)
BOXERS (4036-8)
CANARIES (4611-0)
CATS (4442-8)
CHINCHILLAS (4037-6)
CHOW-CHOWS (3952-1)
CICHLIDS (4597-1)
COCKATIELS (4610-2)
COCKATOOS (4159-3)
CONURES (4880-6)
DACHSHUNDS (1843-5)
DALMATIANS (4605-0)
DISCUS FISH (4669-2)
DOBERMAN PINSCHERS (2999-2)
DOGS (4822-9)
DWARF RABBITS (1352-2)
ENGLISH SPRINGER SPANIELS (1778-1)
FEEDING AND SHELTERING BACKYARD
    BIRDS (4252-2)
FEEDING AND SHELTERING EUROPEAN
    BIRDS (2858-9)
FERRETS (2976-3)
GERBILS (3725-1)
GERMAN SHEPHERDS (2982-8)
GOLDEN RETRIEVERS (3793-6)
GOLDFISH (2975-5)
GOULDIAN FINCHES (4523-8)
GUINEA PIGS (4612-9)
HAMSTERS (4439-8)
IRISH SETTERS (4663-3)
KEESHONDEN (1560-6)
KILLIFISH (4475-4)
LABRADOR RETRIEVERS (3792-8)
LHASA APSOS (3950-5)
LIZARDS IN THE TERRARIUM (3925-4)
LONGHAIRED CATS (2803-1)
LONG-TAILED PARAKEETS (1351-4)
LORIES AND LORIKEETS (1567-3)
LOVEBIRDS (3726-X)

MACAWS (4768-0)
MICE (2921-6)
MINIATURE PIGS (1356-5)
MUTTS (4126-7)
MYNAHS (3688-3)
PARAKEETS (4437-1)
PARROTS (4823-7)
PERSIAN CATS (4405-3)
PIGEONS (4044-9)
POMERANIANS (4670-6)
PONIES (2856-2)
POODLES (2812-0)
RABBITS (4440-1)
RATS (4535-1)
ROTTWEILERS (4483-5)
SCHNAUZERS (3949-1)
SHAR-PEI (4334-2)
SHEEP (4091-0)
SHETLAND SHEEPDOGS (4264-6)
SHIH TZUS (4524-6)
SIAMESE CATS (4764-8)
SIBERIAN HUSKIES (4265-4)
SNAKES (2813-9)
SPANIELS (2424-9)
TROPICAL FISH (4700-1)
TURTLES (4702-8)
YORKSHIRE TERRIERS (4406-1)
ZEBRA FINCHES (3497-X)

NEW PET HANDBOOKS

Detailed, illustrated profiles (40–60 color photos), 144 pp., paperback.

NEW AQUARIUM FISH HANDBOOK
    (3682-4)
NEW AUSTRALIAN PARAKEET
    HANDBOOK (4739-7)
NEW BIRD HANDBOOK (4157-7)
NEW CANARY HANDBOOK (4879-2)
NEW CAT HANDBOOK (2922-4)
NEW COCKATIEL HANDBOOK (4201-8)
NEW DOG HANDBOOK (2857-0)
NEW DUCK HANDBOOK (4088-0)
NEW FINCH HANDBOOK (2859-7)
NEW GOAT HANDBOOK (4090-2)
NEW PARAKEET HANDBOOK (2985-2)
NEW PARROT HANDBOOK (3729-4)
NEW RABBIT HANDBOOK (4202-6)

NEW SALTWATER AQUARIUM
    HANDBOOK (4482-7)
NEW SOFTBILL HANDBOOK (4075-9)
NEW TERRIER HANDBOOK (3951-3)

REFERENCE BOOKS

Comprehensive, lavishly illustrated references (60–300 color photos), 136–176 pp., hardcover & paperback.

AQUARIUM FISH (1350-6)
AQUARIUM FISH BREEDING (4474-6)
AQUARIUM FISH SURVIVAL MANUAL
    (5686-8)
AQUARIUM PLANTS MANUAL (1687-4)
BEFORE YOU BUY THAT PUPPY (1750-1)
BEST PET NAME BOOK EVER, THE
    (4258-1)
CARING FOR YOUR SICK CAT (1726-9)
CAT CARE MANUAL (5765-1)
CIVILIZING YOUR PUPPY (4953-5)
COMMUNICATING WITH YOUR DOG
    (4203-4)
COMPLETE BOOK OF BUDGERIGARS
    (6059-8)
COMPLETE BOOK OF CAT CARE (4613-7)
COMPLETE BOOK OF DOG CARE (4158-5)
COMPLETE BOOK OF PARROTS (5971-9)
DOG CARE MANUAL (5764-3)
FEEDING YOUR PET BIRD (1521-3)
GOLDFISH AND ORNAMENTAL CARP
    (5634-5)
GUIDE TO A WELL BEHAVED CAT
    (1476-6)
GUIDE TO HOME PET GROOMING
    (4298-0)
HEALTHY DOG, HAPPY DOG (1842-7)
HOP TO IT: A Guide to Training Your Pet
    Rabbit (4551-3)
HORSE CARE MANUAL (5795-3)
HOW TO TALK TO YOUR CAT (1749-8)
HOW TO TEACH YOUR OLD DOG
    NEW TRICKS (4544-0)
LABYRINTH FISH (5635-3)
MACAWS (6073-3)
NONVENOMOUS SNAKES (5632-9)
WATER PLANTS IN THE AQUARIUM
    (3926-2)

Barron's Educational Series, Inc. • 250 Wireless Blvd., Hauppauge, NY 11788
Call toll-free: 1-800-645-3476 • In Canada: Georgetown Book Warehouse
34 Armstrong Ave., Georgetown, Ont. L7G 4R9 • Call toll-free: 1-800-247-7160
ISBN prefix: 0-8120 • Order from your favorite book or pet store

BARRON'S

R 2/94